Napoleon

SEMINAR STUDIES IN HISTORY

Napoleon
Conquest, Reform and Reorganisation

CLIVE EMSLEY

PEARSON
Longman

Harlow, England • London • New York • Boston • San Francisco • Toronto • Sydney • Singapore • Hong Kong
Tokyo • Seoul • Taipei • New Delhi • Cape Town • Madrid • Mexico City • Amsterdam • Munich • Paris • Milan

PEARSON EDUCATION LIMITED

Edinburgh Gate
Harlow CM20 2JE
Tel: +44 (0)1279 623623
Fax: +44 (0)1279 431059
Website: www.pearsoned.co.uk

First published in Great Britain in 2003

ISBN 978-0-582-43795-1

British Library Cataloguing in Publication Data
A CIP catalogue record for this book can be obtained from the British Library

Library of Congress Cataloging in Publication Data
A CIP catalog record for this book can be obtained from the Library of Congress

10 9 8 7 6 5
12 11 10 09 08

Typeset by 7 in 10/12 Sabon Roman
Produced by Pearson Education Asia Pte Ltd.
Printed and bound in Malaysia, PA

The Publishers' policy is to use paper manufactured from sustainable forests.

CONTENTS

INTRODUCTION TO THE SERIES

Such is the pace of historical enquiry in the modern world that there is an ever-widening gap between the specialist article or monograph, incorporating the results of current research, and general surveys, which inevitably become out of date. *Seminar Studies in History* is designed to bridge this gap. The series was founded by Patrick Richardson in 1966 and his aim was to cover major themes in British, European and world history. Between 1980 and 1996 Roger Lockyer continued his work, before handing the editorship over to Clive Emsley and Gordon Martel. Clive Emsley is Professor of History at the Open University, while Gordon Martel is Professor of International History at the University of Northern British Columbia, Canada, and Senior Research Fellow at De Montfort University.

All the books are written by experts in their field who are not only familiar with the latest research but have often contributed to it. They are frequently revised, in order to take account of new information and interpretations. They provide a selection of documents to illustrate major themes and provoke discussion, and also a guide to further reading. The aim of *Seminar Studies in History* is to clarify complex issues without over-simplifying them, and to stimulate readers into deepening their knowledge and understanding of major themes and topics.

ACKNOWLEDGEMENTS

We are grateful to the following for permission to reproduce copyright material:

Table 1 based on table in Les 'Masses de granit': cent mille notables de Premier Empire, published and reprinted by permission of Éditions EHESS (Bergeron, L. and Chaussinand-Nogaret, G. 1979); Maps 1 and 2 after maps in Napoleon's Integration of Europe, published and reprinted by permission of Routledge (Woolf, S. 1991); Table 2 adapted from table in France Under Napoleon, translated by R.R. Palmer, copyright © 1981 by Princeton University Press, reprinted by permission of Princeton University Press (Bergeron, L. 1981).

Plate 1 © Photo RMN, Hervé Lewandowski; Plate 2 © Photo RMN, Harry Bréjat; Plate 3 © Photo RMN, Daniel Arnaudet, reprinted by permission of RMN Photo Agency; Plate 4, Samuel H. Kress Collection, Image © 2003 Board of Trustees, National Gallery of Art, Washington, reprinted by permission of National Gallery of Art, Washington.

In some instances we have been unable to trace the owners of copyright material, and we would appreciate any information that would enable us to do so.

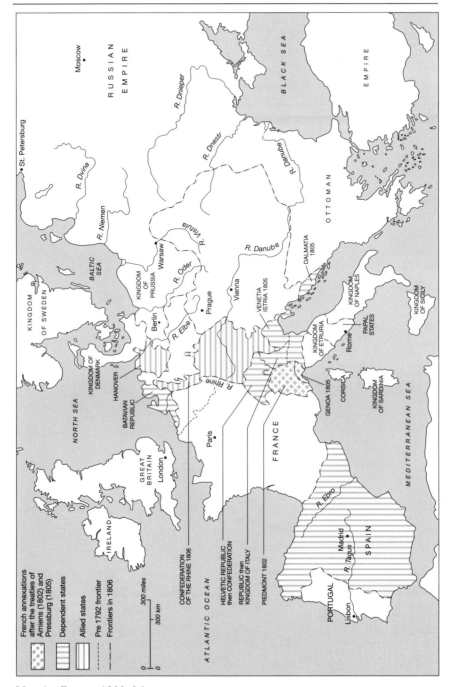

Map 1   Europe 1800–06
Source: After Woolf, S. (1991) *Napoleon's Integration of Europe*; published and
reprinted by permission of Routledge.

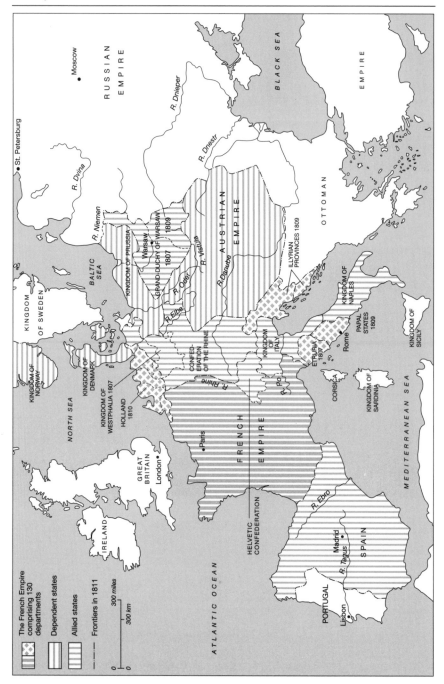

Map 2   Europe 1807–12
Source: After Woolf, S. (1991) *Napoleon's Integration of Europe*, published and
reprinted by permission of Routledge.

CHRONOLOGY

The French Revolutionary Calendar (see page 127) was in use from 1793 (Year II of Liberty) until the end of 1805. This chronology gives the dates from the Revolutionary Calendar where they are most commonly used in histories of the Napoleonic period.

1769
15 August   Napoleone Buonaparte born, Ajaccio, Corsica.

1779
April   N. enters military academy at Brienne.

1784
October   N. enters École Militaire.

1785
22 September   N. commissioned as lieutenant.

1789–93
September–April   N. divides time between Corsica and France.

1793
September–
   December   Siege of Toulon.

1794
July–August   N. briefly imprisoned following the fall of Robespierre.

1795
5 October   [13 *Vendémiaire* Year IV] N. suppresses royalist rising in Paris with 'a whiff of grapeshot'.

1796
23 February   N. given command of the Army of Italy.
9 March   N. marries Josephine de Beauharnais.

26 March	N. takes command in Italy. Successful campaign winning Lodi (11 May), Castiglione (5 August), Arcola (15–17 October).

1797

14 January	Battle of Rivoli, leading to peace preliminaries of Leoben (18 April) and Peace of Campo Formio (17 October) with Austria.
9 July	N. establishes Cisalpine Republic.
9 December	N. takes command of the Army of England.

1798

19 May	N. sails for Egypt – Lands 1 July, Battle of the Pyramids (21 July).

1799

April	Coalition organised against France (Austria, Britain, Russia).
9 October	N. returns to France.
9–10 November	[18–19 *Brumaire* Year VIII] Coup of *Brumaire*, Consulate established.
15 December	[24 *Frimaire* Year VIII] Constitution of Year VIII (approved by plebiscite Jan. 1800).
28 December	Sunday services recommence in churches.

1800

17 February	[28 *Pluviôse* Year VIII] Law of 28 *Pluviôse* establishes departmental prefects and new administrative system for France.
14 June	Battle of Marengo.
20 October	List of prescribed *émigrés* is modified to enable more to return to France.

1801

9 February	Peace of Lunéville with Austria.

1802

25 March	Peace of Amiens with Britain.
8 April	Concordat published.
19 May	*Légion d'honneur* established.
2 August	[14 *Thermidor* Year X] Plebiscite confirms N. Consul for Life.
4 August	Constitution of Year X.

1803

18 May	Rupture of the Peace of Amiens. By end of year the Army of England is massing around Boulogne ready to invade Britain.

1804

20 March	Kidnap and execution of duc d'Enghien.
21 March	Civil Code promulgated.
18 May	[28 *Floréal* Year XII] Senate proclaims N. 'Emperor of the French', leading to new plebiscite to approve the empire.
10 August	Francis II (Holy Roman Emperor) assumes title of hereditary emperor of Austria, becoming Francis I. Essentially this means the dissolution of the Holy Roman Empire.
2 December	[11 *Frimaire* Year XIII] N. crowns himself and Josephine in the Cathedral of Notre Dame in Paris.

1805

26 May	N. crowned King of Italy in Milan.
August	Coalition organised against France (Austria, Britain, Russia).
24 August	Camp at Boulogne broken up. N. marches east.
20 October	Austrian army surrenders at Ulm.
21 October	Nelson defeats Franco-Spanish fleet at Trafalgar.
2 December	Battle of Austerlitz, Austria sues for peace leading to Peace of Pressburg.
	(26 December), Russia withdraws.
31 December	[10 *Nivôse* Year XIV] Termination of the Revolutionary Calendar.

1806

Spring–Summer	N. reorganises much of Europe creating brothers Kings of Naples (Joseph) and Holland (Louis).
June	N. abolishes Holy Roman Empire.
12 July	N. establishes Confederation of the Rhine.
September	War against Prussia.
14 October	Battles of Jena and Auerstadt.
21 October	Berlin Decree to blockade Britain.
10 December	Opening of Grand Sanhedrin, which leads to (2 March 1807) decrees on the civil status of Jews in the empire.

1807

8 February	Battle of Eylau.

14 June	Battle of Friedland.
25 June	N. meets Tsar Alexander at Tilsit, leading to Treaties of Tilsit (7–9 July).
8 August	Jerome Bonaparte King of Westphalia.
17 December	Milan Decree strengthens blockade of Britain.

1808

2 February	French troops invade Rome and Spain, former leads to Pius VII excommunicating N. (27 March).
1 March	Two decrees systematising the new imperial nobility.
2 May	Rising in Madrid against French troops.
10 May	At Bayonne Charles IV and Ferdinand VII of Spain forced to cede their rights to N., leading to Joseph Bonaparte becoming King of Spain and Marshal Murat King of Naples.
September– October	N. meets Tsar Alexander at Erfurt. Tilsit Treaty renewed.

1809

April	Austria joins Britain in war against N.
17 May	Papal states annexed to France; N. excommunicated a second time (10 June); Pius VII arrested (6 July).
6 July	Battle of Wagram.
27–28 June	Battle of Talavera – Wellesley defeats King Joseph and Marshal Victor.
14 October	Peace of Schönbrunn.
16 December	Divorce of Josephine.

1810

1 April	Marriage of N. and Marie Louise solemnized at Saint Cloud.
9 July	Holland annexed to France.

1811

20 March	Birth of the King of Rome.

1812

24 June	Grand Army crosses Nieman River, Moscow campaign begins.
22 July	Battle of Salamanca – Wellington defeats Marshal Marmont. Joseph has to quit Madrid.
7 September	Battle of Borodino.
14 September	French enter Moscow.

19 October	French withdraw from Moscow.
22–23 October	Conspiracy of General Malet.
25–29 November	French fight their way across the Berezina River.
18 December	N. reaches Paris.

failure in Russia inspires formation of the Sixth Coalition.

1813

February–March	Alliances of Austria, Britain, Prussia, Russia and Sweden against France.

May → Napo. victorious at Lützen & Bautzen.

21 June	Battle of Vittoria – Wellington defeats Joseph. Joseph leaves Spain. N. replaces him with Marshal Soult.
26 July–1 August	Battle of the Pyrenees – Wellington defeats Soult and pursues him crossing into France (November).
16–19 October	Battle of Leipzig.

1814

1 January	Prussian troops cross the Rhine beginning the campaign in Northern France.
30–31 March	Paris falls to allied troops.
3 April	Senate votes dethronement of N. He abdicates (6 April) in favour of the King of Rome. This is rejected, the King of Rome is taken to Austria and gets new title of Duke of Reichstadt.
3 May	N. lands on Elba.
September	Congress of Vienna convenes.

1815

1 March	N. lands back in France, marches to Paris (arrives 20 March).
22 April	Promulgation of the *Acte additionnelle*.
16–18 June	Three days of fighting in Belgium culminates in the battle of Waterloo.
22 June	N. abdicates for second time, surrendering to British (15 July).
17 October	N. lands on St Helena.

1821

5 May	Death of N.

1840

15 December	N.'s remains, having been brought back to France, are interred in Les Invalides, Paris.

PART ONE   INTRODUCTION

CHAPTER ONE

'MY HISTORY IS MADE UP OF FACTS, AND WORDS ALONE CANNOT DESTROY THEM'

Commenting on his detractors to the comte de Las Cases in his lonely exile upon St Helena, Napoleon was right to stress that facts had made up his career. Nevertheless, while words might not destroy these facts, they have to be used to describe the facts and to express interpretations of the facts. In his conversations with Las Cases, and with others, Napoleon spent a considerable amount of time interpreting the facts of his career for posterity. In precisely the same way, supporters of the Bourbon monarchy that was restored to France after his fall, and the chroniclers of the states that contributed to that fall, as well as subsequent generations of historians, have all described, interpreted and re-interpreted the very same facts. As Napoleon also said, with some justice, in Las Cases's hearing: 'Every body has loved me and hated me: every one has been for me and against me by turns. I may truly say there is not a single Frenchman in whom I have not excited interest.' And the interest was not restricted, and has not remained restricted to the people of France.

Probably no other single individual had such a profound impact on the development of modern France and on that of nineteenth-century Europe as Napoleon Bonaparte. The sheer scale of his military success and eventual disaster, the scale of his administrative and governmental changes, and of his redrawing of European frontiers, all served to generate strong feelings during his lifetime. Subsequently they have all contributed to him becoming a figure of controversy among historians and among others who find in his career contemporary parallels or the roots of many contemporary issues. Napoleon contributed to these controversies himself. From his earliest campaigns he consciously manipulated his image and information about himself. In exile he glossed his career in the memoirs that he dictated, principally to Las Cases, and in the comments that he made about his career to others. This gloss was burnished by the commission established in 1854 by his nephew, Napoleon III, to collect and publish his correspondence. The commission's expressed aim was to publish in accordance with the image that Napoleon wished to project of himself. And while the 32 volumes that appeared as a result of the commission's work have proved to be an invaluable source for historians, the expressed aim led to a variety of omissions and exclusions of which some historians have been more aware than others (Thompson, 1998: ix–xi). Yet, even if Napoleon worked carefully at his image, and even though his supporters and successors worked similarly, there can be no gainsaying his personal charisma and the qualities that inspired his followers and his soldiers, and, at the end, even won over some of his captors.

Biography is not greatly favoured by modern academic historians and several of the best books of this sort tend to focus less on Napoleon the man and more on his impact on France (Ellis, 1997; Lyons, 1994; Tulard, 1984 are all good examples). Recent biographies focusing more specifically on the man still become entangled in early nineteenth-century debates as to whether he was essentially a force for good or evil, and/or have often tended to seek explanations for his behaviour rooted in, for example, Freudian psychology. Moreover, once an author becomes entangled in such issues there is the further problem of trying to establish the subject's overall aims and objectives, as well as the intentions at different moments of a career. For example, did Napoleon have a genuine vision for France, and for Europe? At what point did he decide that he had the ability and the opportunity to take control of France? At what point, if at all in his career, might he have been prepared to hang up his sword and cease fighting? Were his personality and ambitions the principal cause of the Napoleonic wars? Or were his apparently endless wars forced on him by jealous rivals, and especially by the government in London that constituted his most persistent enemy, funded coalition after coalition against him until his second abdication in 1815, and guarded him in his lonely exile on St Helena? The debates between nineteenth- and early twentieth-century French historians on these issues have been superbly explored by the Dutch historian Pieter Geyl. He might have broadened his coverage to include at least British, Dutch, German, Italian, Spanish and Russian historians, though these would, probably, have been rather more 'against' than 'for'. Also, while Geyl was writing more than half a century ago, his point was well made that 'History is indeed an argument without end', and especially with reference to Napoleon (Geyl, 1949: 18). More recently R.S. Alexander has broadened the geographical range of Napoleonic historiography with a new analysis and has brought it up to date. Alexander suggests, further, that part of the problem with the history of Napoleon is that, while there remain occasional lacunae, there simply is so much that is known about him. Moreover, since Napoleon was both a great publicist and a great opportunist, his words and deeds have enabled his career to be interpreted and re-interpreted, as well as hitched to a variety of nineteenth- and twentieth-century political 'isms' (Alexander, 2001). There were moments in his career when he appeared to be a liberal, and others when he was the dictatorial tyrant; he continued the reforms of the Revolution, but his perception of society and of how it should be structured was fundamentally conservative.

What follows is designed as a broad introduction first, to Napoleon's career, achievements and legacy, and second to some of the debates about, and interpretations of his career. The core of the book is divided into three principal chapters. The first of these briefly chronicles Napoleon's career. Chapters Three and Four survey, respectively, his impact on France and on Europe. A short concluding chapter discusses some of the lasting effects of his career and achievements. The final quarter of the book is made up of Documents selected to illustrate some of the events and issues explored in the main text, as well as some of the complexities involved in assessing Napoleon's career, achievements and legacy. There is also a Glossary, a brief Who's Who, and a Chronology of some of the key events.

PART TWO

CHAPTER TWO

THE CAREER AND THE MAN

MAKING A NAME

More by accident than design the French Revolution produced a clutch of able young generals. In the early years of the Revolution a few military officers, drawn from the scions of the nobility, emigrated. When war began against the crowned heads of Europe, and when France became a republic, still more left. Those that remained saw their numbers diminish in action on the battlefield or in purges – sometimes because of military failure, sometimes because they were politically suspect, and sometimes they appear simply to have been fingered as necessary scapegoats. Into their shoes stepped a few men who, in the royal army, could rarely, if ever, have risen above the rank of non-commissioned officer. Lazare Hoche, born in 1768, began life as a stable-boy, was a corporal in 1789, and a general four years later. Michel Ney, born in 1769, was the son of a cooper. He enlisted as a hussar in 1788, was made a lieutenant at the beginning of war in 1792, and became a general in 1796. At the same time, young officers of the old regime army, who came from the nobility, showed loyalty to the Revolution, ability on the battlefield, and made the right connections, also found rapid promotion. One such was Napoleon Bonaparte.

Napoleone Buonaparte (the original spelling of his name) was born in Corsica in 1769, the year after the island had been transferred to French rule by the Italian state of Genoa. He was the second son of a family that claimed Italian noble blood. His father, Carlo (or Charles), had rallied rapidly to the French and had secured recognition of the family's claim to noble rank. Accounts of Napoleone's childhood are rare and unreliable. What is certain is that his father seized the opportunity of rewards offered by Louis XVI to his loyal Corsican nobility, and this enabled Napoleone, and his elder brother Joseph, to be educated in France. After five years at the military academy in Brienne, Napoleone transferred to the *École Militaire* in Paris in 1784, and was gazetted as an artillery officer the following year (Carrington, 1986; Parker, 2001). The artillery was a technical arm. It was not one of the glamorous guards or cavalry regiments of the old regime army and it was unlikely that a young officer of relatively lowly origins, and with a pronounced Corsican accent, would have risen to the greatest military rank, but then came revolution and war.

In the early stages of the Revolution Napoleone returned to Corsica and was elected Lieutenant Colonel in the local National Guard. During his years at military school and as a young officer, he appears to have developed a world view and a personal identity based on a romantic imagining of the island of his birth. In particular he idolised the Corsican patriot leader Pasquale Paoli. Once back in Corsica, however, the idealised picture of his homeland rapidly evaporated. For some time his family had been feuding with Paoli, and in 1793 the entire Buonaparte family was compelled to flee to France. Once back in France Napoleone rejoined the army and transformed himself into a Jacobin revolutionary (Dwyer, 2002). Captain Buonaparte showed courage and ability in commanding the artillery at the siege of Toulon in December 1793 and was promoted to general. But, the following summer, his links with the Jacobins led to him being briefly imprisoned on the fall of Robespierre. During 1795 he hovered in the corridors of power in Paris seeking a command. There he became particularly close to the corrupt, unscrupulous, but politically adept, Paul Barras. On 5 October 1795, working under Barras's direction, he was available in Paris to command some of the troops who swept away the Royalist rising of *Vendémiaire* with 'a whiff of grapeshot'. Five days later he was appointed commander of the Army of the Interior. He maintained close links with members of the new government, the Directory, established in November, in which Barras was to remain prominent. On 9 March 1796 he married Barras's former mistress, Josephine de Beauharnais, who was six years his senior. Two days later he left to take up a new command, the Army of Italy.

It was in Italy that Citizen General Napoleon Bonaparte – his name now without its Corsican spelling – began to make a significant mark. In the twelve months from April 1796 he fought a brilliant campaign against the Austrians in Italy bringing them to sign the preliminary Peace of Leoben on 19 April 1797. He established, under his own presidency and according to his own ideas, sister republics in the north of the peninsula (the Cispadane in 1796 which was expanded into the Cisalpine in 1797, and the Ligurian, also in 1797). He imposed a treaty on the Papacy, and subsequently (May 1797) occupied the Venetian Republic. He sent artistic treasures and cash indemnities back to his political masters in Paris. In September 1797, at Barras's request for assistance, he sent his deputy commander, General Augereau, to provide military support for the *coup d'état* of 18 *Fructidor* Year V (4 September). But it was also clear that General Bonaparte was increasingly becoming his own man with his own agenda. Many of his actions were taken without reference to the Directory. The Peace of Leoben was negotiated with little regard for the instructions sent from Paris, so too was the follow-up Treaty of Campo Formio (18 October 1797) whereby General Bonaparte, now playing the diplomat in addition to the soldier, secured the French occupation of Belgium, the recognition of the Ligurian Republic, and ceded Venice to Austria. His creation of sister republics gave him his first taste of political leadership and of establishing institutions of State – experiences that none of his military rivals shared. At the same time Bonaparte was beginning to develop his own legend. His victories at Lodi (10 May 1796), Arcola (15–18 November 1796) and Rivoli (14 January 1797) were impressive, but they were made all the more spectacular by carefully crafted reports in the newspapers founded for the Army of Italy; and these newspapers were also distributed in France.

At the close of his successful campaign in Italy Bonaparte appeared to be the most successful of the young generals (see *Doc. 1*). The man who might have become his most serious rival, the Jacobin Lazare Hoche, had died of consumption two weeks after the *Fructidor* coup. In October 1797 he was appointed to command the army designated for the invasion of England, the French Republic's last remaining enemy. But Bonaparte was wary of the invasion scheme. The difficulties of such a venture had been demonstrated by Hoche's aborted expedition to Ireland the previous December, and Britain's Royal Navy remained a serious threat to any military attempt to cross the Channel. Yet the alternative expedition on which Bonaparte eventually embarked, an invasion of Egypt, was every bit as risky. The Egyptian adventure, with its accompanying train of scientists and savants, provided romance and victories for the Napoleonic legend. It also led to significant intellectual progress, not the least of which was the discovery of the Rosetta stone which provided the key for deciphering the monuments of ancient Egypt. But if it was ultimately a military disaster, it was not known as such in France until long after General Bonaparte's return. Moreover, it had kept Bonaparte away from the coups and purges that continued to undermine the Directory during 1798 and 1799, and from the military reverses that marked the renewed hostilities with Austria early in 1799. As a result, when he returned to France with a small group of men in October 1799, General Bonaparte could pose as an untainted military saviour who could bring order out of chaos and victory out of defeat. And for the group of politicians plotting a parliamentary coup with the aim of creating a faction-free, properly functioning political system, he seemed to be the ideal sword for cowering opponents.

In itself the *coup d'état* of 18–19 *Brumaire* Year VIII (9–10 November 1799) was not a particularly exceptional coup. General Bonaparte did not distinguish himself personally, allowing his impatience to encourage him into a foolish and almost disastrous hectoring of the Directory's largest legislative chamber, the Council of Five Hundred. The result, however, was to prove significant. It brought to an end the five-man executive Directory and saw the creation of the three-man Consulate. The three provisional consuls who took over in the aftermath of the coup were Roger Ducos, a Jacobin lawyer who had served as a Director since June 1799, Emmanuel-Joseph Sieyès, a former priest, revolutionary pamphleteer and deputy, who had been elected as a Director in May 1799, and Bonaparte.

MASTERING FRANCE

In recent years historians have begun to reassess the Directory and to see within it the seeds of some of the reforms later claimed as the work of Bonaparte. Yet, as they would readily acknowledge, this is done with the benefit of hindsight. The Directory was unpopular and the conspirators of *Brumaire* knew this. It had failed to bring an end to the interminable wars of the Revolution; and even more serious, especially in the eyes of those men of property who had profited from the early upheavals of the Revolution, it had failed to establish internal security. The Directory had been prone to coup and counter-coup in Paris, while in the provinces royalist counter-revolution still posed a threat in the west, and brigandage was rife in the south. The first task of the *Brumaire* conspirators was the preparation of a new constitution that would bring an end to the political chaos of the Directory and establish firm executive leadership. They wanted to preserve the essence of the Revolution, but to steer a course between the political excesses of Jacobinism and royalism.

Much of the new constitution was the work of Sieyès who envisaged a Great Elector as the dominant figure of the new system. In the event, however, the title of consul was maintained. Of the three consuls, one was to hold principal executive power appointing the officers of State, and the two others were to act in a consultative capacity. Bonaparte held the post of First Consul. Sieyès, though central in drafting the system, declared himself unwilling to act as the general's aide de camp and Ducos also stepped aside to work with Sieyès in the newly created Senate. The two replacement consuls designated to work alongside Bonaparte, and essentially his choice, were Jean-Jacques Régis de Cambacérès, a former noble who had followed a legal career before the Revolution and acted as a Jacobin deputy during it, and Charles-François Lebrun, a royal administrator before the Revolution, possibly still a royalist at heart, but well known as a moderate. The political mix of consuls reflected an attempt to bring reconciliation among political opponents of the preceding decade. They were also indicative of General Bonaparte's ability to pick able and loyal subordinates. Lebrun, aged 61 at the time of *Brumaire*, was to become Arch-Treasurer to the Empire on its creation in 1804 and subsequently acted as Governor of Liguria (1805–06) and Governor General of the Dutch provinces annexed to France in 1810. Cambacérès was sixteen years younger and he rose to even loftier heights.

In the words of Isser Woloch, he became 'the second most powerful man in Napoleonic France ... warming Napoleon's chair' when the latter was away on campaign. As Arch-Chancellor of the Empire, during Napoleon's absences he monitored the legislature, organised weekly meetings of ministers, coordinated their work, and sent regular reports to the Emperor (Woloch, 2001a, ch. V).

Bonaparte himself played an active role in the discussions that resulted in the new constitution; he was, after all, no stranger to such discussions having played a key role in the creation of first the Cispadane, and then the larger Cisalpine Republic in Italy. Even so, it is difficult to know with any certainty who was responsible for specific details. The Constitution of Year VIII provided for a centralised, top-down control of legislation and of administrative and legislative appointments. This might smack of a military system favourable to General Bonaparte, yet it also followed a pattern detectable throughout the Revolution of electoral freedoms, that had rarely gone much beyond rhetoric and promises, being progressively curtailed. The Constitution of Year VIII had no introductory statement regarding the rights of citizens, though it did promise the inviolability of the home. It accepted universal manhood suffrage, but filtered this through a succession of elective rounds: the primary electorate of about 6 million men chose communal electors; these, in turn, selected departmental electors who, in turn, presented a national list of 6000 men. It was from the latter list that the Senate was to select 100 men aged over 25 for the Tribunate and 300 men aged at least 30 for the Legislative Body. The Tribunate was to discuss legislation; the Legislative Body was to vote on proposed legislation. However, neither of these bodies was to initiate legislation; this was to be the task of the Senate or the Consuls, and after a few years, particularly once the various legal codes were voted through, the legislature was increasingly sidelined.

The Senate was to have 80 members, aged 40 years or more. It began with Sieyès and Ducos who were to select 29 senators; the 31 were then to select another 29, and to co-opt another two each year for the next ten years. Members of the Senate were appointed for life. However one-fifth of the members of the legislative bodies were to be replaced annually. There was no clear statement about how these fifths were to be selected, and this gave Bonaparte the opportunity to remove any individuals who created difficulties. In 1802, for example, there was a purge of liberals from the Tribunate, including the removal of such figures as Benjamin Constant and the political economist Jean-Baptiste Say. In addition to this ability to purge the legislature, Bonaparte also rapidly acquired the power of selecting new or replacement senators.

The Constitution provided other opportunities for Bonaparte to acquire and exercise power. The Senate was given the authority to issue decrees (*senatus consulta*) that bypassed the legislature. As the Senate became more compliant to his will, Bonaparte used these decrees to evade any parliamentary opposition. Moreover, the First Consul could choose his own councillors for a new State council, the *Conseil d'État*. The council was to advise the First Consul on administrative and legal matters, and for this he carefully selected men with the appropriate expertise. It was behind the closed doors of the council, that the First Consul and later Emperor, was prepared to debate and to listen to criticism; and it was in the council that the details of legislation were generally hammered out before being forwarded to the talking shop of the Tribunate or to the Senate. General Bonaparte was aware that, in the aftermath of the Revolution, it was not possible to dismiss all appeals to popular sovereignty and to ignore popular opinion. However, once the framework of his government system was established, organised, and running smoothly, Napoleon argued that it was logical for the legislature to give way to administration. What this often meant in practice was that he submitted very general legislative outlines to the deputies and then filled in the details subsequently by executive decree.

While he was not prepared to await the final verdict before pressing forward with adopting the constitution, Bonaparte did have the constitution submitted to a plebiscite. On 18 *Pluviôse* Year VIII (7 February 1800) the government was delighted to announce that 3 million voters had signed their names in support of the constitution while a mere 1562 had declared against it. In reality the Ministry of the Interior, then under the leadership of the First Consul's younger brother Lucien, significantly massaged the figures almost doubling the 'yes' vote not least by including 500,000 votes declared on behalf of the army when the soldiers had never, in fact, been given the opportunity to vote. Yet Bonaparte did gain considerable popular support in the two years following the coup of *Brumaire*; this was a result of his achievements in securing internal order and in making peace with external enemies.

Almost immediately after *Brumaire* Bonaparte sought to bring an end to royalist counter-revolution in the West. There was an armistice, followed by some renewed fighting. Within a year, however, many of the royalist leaders had either been beaten or had given up the struggle, and to hasten matters along Bonaparte made concessions, not least in the reduction of conscription quotas. Tough policies were introduced against brigandage and, even while they were not immediately successful and were not, in any significant respect, greatly different from the policies of the Directory, they appear to have had an important role in restoring confidence. While these moves sought to restore internal order General Bonaparte led an army across the Alps to confront the Austrians in Italy. Again the publicity machine was deployed to ensure that the First Consul got the best coverage even when other generals were also performing well; moreover, errors on the part of the First Consul were ignored while fortunate strokes of luck tended to be portrayed as part of a master plan. The battle of Marengo, fought on 14 June 1800, provides a vivid example. Bonaparte, believing that he had the Austrians on the run, divided his army in pursuit, only to be confronted by an Austrian force twice the size of the force he had kept with him. General Desaix rejoined the army with his division just in time to save the day for the French. Unfortunately for Desaix, he managed to get himself killed in the moment of victory; something which enabled the glory to stay with the First Consul.

The Directory, while not overtly anti-Christian like some of the extreme Jacobins of 1793–94, had never been keen to re-establish links with the Catholic Church. In contrast, just over a week after Marengo, Bonaparte put out feelers to the Pope suggesting that they begin negotiations to put an end to the friction between the French Republic and the Papacy. In little more than a year a Concordat was signed between the First Consul and Pope Pius VII recognising Catholicism as the religion of the majority of Frenchmen but also ensuring the ultimate authority of the French State over the Church. To emphasise this secular supremacy, and without consulting the Pope, Bonaparte added his own Organic Articles to the Concordat when it was finally published (see below, pp. 50–1 and *Docs 4a* and *4b*). However, in spite of this sleight of hand, the Concordat made more problematic any close association between the Catholic Church and the royalist opposition. Modifications were made in the proscription of *émigrés* and by the beginning of 1802 roughly four out of ten of those who had emigrated from Revolutionary France had returned to the new France of the Consulate. A preliminary treaty with the British, the Treaty of London signed on 1 October 1801, brought a cessation of hostilities with the paymaster of France's enemies both internal and external. The Peace of Amiens was agreed the following March.

In two years as First Consul, General Bonaparte had succeeded where his immediate predecessors had signally failed: he had achieved the peace and security that the French people sought after a decade of revolutionary upheaval and war. But he had enemies; royalists and radical Jacobin opponents were still active. On 24 December 1800 a group of royalists attempted to assassinate him with a bomb – 'the infernal machine' – in rue Nicaise in Paris. It was the second attempt in three months. While Joseph Fouché, the Minister of Police, assured him that royalists were to blame for the plot, Bonaparte used the incident as an opportunity to get rid of the potential Jacobin threat. A *senatus consultum* promptly exiled 130 of them; and after this the real royalist conspirators were dealt with.

On the back of these successes Bonaparte took a further step to secure his position as the head of State. A new plebiscite was held and the people were asked to agree to the simple question: 'Should Napoleon Bonaparte be consul for life?' Men – and it must be remembered that the plebiscites only sought male opinion – were simply asked to sign their names in 'yes' or 'no' columns; there was no notion of a secret ballot. Nor was there any suggestion as to whether this life consulship would entail any further changes to political institutions. Almost certainly because of the achievements of the preceding two years the plebiscite of 1802 secured 3,653,600 approval votes, as opposed to 8,272 'noes', and on this occasion there was no significant massaging of the figures. Men sometimes appended comments to their votes and, in 1802, these were largely positive. 'The man who has given us peace, religion and order in such a short space of time', declared one Parisian, 'is the most capable of perpetuating these achievements' (quoted in Crook, 2003: 31). The verdict encouraged Bonaparte to strengthen his power further, particularly over the legislature through a series of *senatus consulta*; indeed, he could now use such decrees to put an interpretation on the constitution or even suspend it. Jean Tulard has drawn attention to the way that the question on this plebiscite expressed the First Consul's name: 'Until now it had been "Citizen Bonaparte" or "General Bonaparte" ... the time was near when he would be called "Napoleon", "Bonaparte" being relegated to obscurity' (Tulard, 1984: 119).

It was another conspiracy that provided the opportunity for establishing the hereditary principle in Bonapartist rule. Towards the end of 1803 a group of royalist plotters were arrested in Paris. Interrogations unearthed an extensive, if poorly planned conspiracy to kidnap or kill the First Consul upon the arrival of a Bourbon prince in France. The leading *Chouan* Georges Cadoudal was arrested, together with Generals Moreau and Pichegru. Cadoudal and eleven others were executed; Moreau was banished; Pichegru was found strangled in his cell. More shocking to international, and even to French opinion, in March 1804 French troops and gendarmes crossed into the German state of Baden and seized the duc d'Enghien, a French nobleman who had served in the *émigré* armies. D'Enghien, alleged to be the Bourbon prince whose arrival would ignite the plot, was taken immediately to the fortress of Vincennes on the outskirts of Paris, tried by a military court, and shot (*Doc. 3*).

During and immediately after these startling events, Bonapartist propaganda posed the questions: what would happen if the First Consul was to be assassinated? Who would assume power? And how? A *senatus consultum* of 28 *Floréal* Year XII (18 May 1804) established a new regime with the Republic entrusted to an emperor. A new plebiscite asked the people to approve 'the hereditary transmission of the imperial dignity through the direct, natural, legitimate and adoptive descent of Napoleon Bonaparte, and the direct, natural and legitimate descent of Joseph Bonaparte and Louis Bonaparte'. There was a decline in the 'yes' vote from 1802: 3,572,329 agreed to the proposal and 2,569 voted against, but this was in an electorate increased by the assimilation of new departments into France. Italians abstained in large numbers. In the Belgian department of Dyle there appeared to be more votes of approval than there were voters, and elsewhere the 'yes' vote was massaged upwards. A few courageous individuals even set out their misgivings on their voting papers. 'The reign of a single person seems to me utterly incompatible with the sovereignty of the people,' wrote one citizen in the department of Aube. 'Bonaparte merits all the honours bestowed upon him, but will his successors inherit the same talents and virtues? I am thus obliged to say no...' (quoted in Crook, 2003: 32). As far as the Bonapartists were concerned, however, the plebiscite's outcome was satisfactory.

On 11 *Frimaire* Year XIII (2 December 1804) the coronation of the new Emperor of the French was held in the Cathedral of Notre Dame in Paris. Pius VII was persuaded to travel from Rome for the ceremony, and he hoped that this would enable him to effect some changes in the Organic Articles. But he was left redundant as Napoleon decided to crown himself and his empress. Conscious of how the scene would look for posterity, Napoleon required the artist Jacques-Louis David to paint the Pope's hand raised in blessing (see Plate 1).

MASTERING EUROPE

The Peace of Amiens had broken down a year and a half before the coronation, and the war against Britain was to continue until Napoleon's downfall. Blame for the breakdown and the continuance of the war has been apportioned to both sides in equal measure. At one extreme there have been British historians who have portrayed Napoleon as a precursor of Hitler, determined to dominate Europe and stifle liberty. At the opposite end of the spectrum have been those historians who have taken a veritable Napoleonic line, critical of 'perfidious Albion' who, jealous of France and French success, financed coalition after coalition to bring her and her Emperor down thus compelling Napoleon and his people to interminable war, when what they wanted was peace.

When the Peace of Amiens ruptured in May 1803, with both sides blaming the other, Napoleon began massing an army on the Channel coast for an invasion. The invasion was never launched, partly, perhaps, because of the sheer problem of crossing 20 or so miles of water opposed by the formidable Royal Navy, but also because of distractions elsewhere. When, on 21 October 1805, Nelson's ships comprehensively defeated the combined fleets of France and her Spanish ally off Cape Trafalgar, Napoleon had already swung his army from the Channel to confront the Austrians and Russians in central Europe. The Austrians and Russians had become suspicious of Napoleon's policies in Italy, particularly the annexation of Piedmont and transformation of the Italian Republic into a Napoleonic

he King of Prussia, Frederick William III, equally suspicious of
t generally fearful of war, was bought off with the promise of
...ii monarch's German province of Hanover. The Austrians and
Russians remained resolute and, assured of British subsidies, they prepared
armies for the field. But, in a lightning campaign Napoleon compelled a
massive Austrian surrender at Ulm (22 November), occupied Vienna (15
November), defeated combined Austrian and Russian forces at Austerlitz
(2 December), and crowned his success with the Peace of Pressburg (26
December). By the terms of the latter Austria recognised the changes in Italy
and ceded territory to the swollen principalities of Baden, Bavaria and
Württemberg that Napoleon was fostering in southern Germany.

Early in 1806 Napoleon began several months of unsuccessful negotiations with the British. He also began cementing his alliances in Germany
with dynastic marriages. His stepson, Eugène de Beauharnais, married the
daughter of the King of Bavaria; his wife's niece, Stephanie de Beauharnais,
married the heir to the Grand Duchy of Baden; his brother Jerome was
compelled to give up an American bride, the mother of his baby son, and
was betrothed to the daughter of the King of Württemberg. In the summer
he brought his German allies and satellites together in the Confederation of
the Rhine (*Doc.* 7), an alliance that alarmed Prussia. Prussia was in the
process of finalising the annexation of Hanover, and rumours of attempts by
Napoleon to secure a peace with Britain by promising the return of Hanover
to the British monarchy, aggravated her concerns. Frederick William's
Prussia had sought to sit on the sidelines and pick up spoils from the wars
of others, but she now found herself pushed into a corner. Her attempt to
create a north German equivalent of the Confederation of the Rhine was
blocked by Napoleon. She renewed a defensive alliance with Russia and
resolved on war. Her armies were decisively defeated in the dual battle of
Jena-Auerstädt on 14 October 1806. Russia continued to fight.

The inconclusive battle of Eylau was fought in a snowstorm in February
1807. In June Napoleon beat the Russians at Friedland, and in the following
month Tsar Alexander met Napoleon on a raft in the River Nieman at Tilsit.
Alexander was prepared to accept Napoleon's promises of letting Russia
grow at the expense of Sweden and, especially, the Ottoman Empire. He was
also prepared to join the blockade of British goods in the belief that this
would force Britain to sue for peace and ease Napoleon's pressure on
Europe. But in return for Napoleon's promises, Alexander made concrete
concessions. Russia lost no territory herself by the Treaties of Tilsit. However, by these treaties Alexander agreed to Napoleon's emasculation of
Prussia, to his changes in Naples, where his brother Joseph had been made
king in March 1806, in Holland, where his brother Louis had been made
king in June 1806, and elsewhere in Germany, where a new kingdom of
Westphalia was established for his brother Jerome.

In the summer of 1807 Napoleon was at the height of his influence in Europe. All of the principal continental powers had been defeated and were in some way allied to him. In addition, the rulers of a cluster of smaller states such as Holland, the states of southern Germany and the principalities of Italy were members of, or linked to, his family, and/or owed the structure of their territories and even their very existence to his success. The problem of Britain remained, but Napoleon hoped that through an economic block-ade he could force her to sue for peace. The blockade had begun with the Berlin Decree issued on 21 November 1806 forbidding all parts of Europe under French control from buying either British goods or goods carried in British ships. It was strengthened by the Milan Decrees (23 November and 17 December 1806) which threatened the seizure of any ship that put into a British port or complied with the British counter-measures (*Doc. 13*). To make such a system work Napoleon had to plug any gaps, and through this he became embroiled in war on the Iberian peninsula.

In 1807 Portugal appeared to constitute the major leak in the Contin-ental Blockade and Napoleon decided on an invasion to bring that country into line. But invading Portugal meant marching imperial troops through Spain. Spain was an ally of Napoleon, but an uncertain one. The principal minister, Godoy, had been negotiating an alliance with Prussia in 1806. To Napoleon, the heir to the Spanish throne, Ferdinand, had appeared to be a more reliable bet than his father and the chief minister. Indeed, Ferdinand and his supporters had been putting out feelers and suggesting the possibility of marriage to a Bonaparte bride, when Godoy and King Charles IV had the prince arrested towards the end of 1807. In February 1808 the family feud in Spain took a new turn when a popular uprising, spearheaded by Royal Guards, replaced Charles with Ferdinand. Independently of each other both Charles and Ferdinand appealed to Napoleon to mediate between them, but this proved to be a fatal mistake. When all three met at Bayonne early in May 1808 Napoleon became exasperated with both father and son. By then the occupation of Portugal was well advanced and imperial troops sup-porting those in Portugal were established in considerable numbers in Spain. Napoleon concluded that the best means of securing his southern flank, together with the additional bonus of acquiring the treasure of Spanish America, was to replace both Charles and Ferdinand with one of his brothers. In consequence Charles and Ferdinand were compelled to abdicate in favour of Joseph Bonaparte.

In July 1808 Joseph was crowned king of Spain, while his former kingdom, Naples, was handed to Napoleon's insatiable youngest sister, Caroline, and her husband, the flamboyant cavalry commander, Joachim Murat. The exchange in Naples passed off peacefully, but the Spanish people had been in revolt against Napoleon's occupying army since May. For the next five years thousands of French imperial troops were to confront regular

Spanish armies, Spanish guerrillas and an Anglo-Portuguese army under Sir Arthur Wellesley – later the Duke of Wellington – in a merciless struggle for the country. The 'Spanish ulcer' proved to be a constant drain on men and matériel, yet Napoleon himself never set foot in the country after fighting a brief, ostensibly successful campaign at the close of 1808, and whether through pride or because of the mountain of other, more immediate issues that filled his agenda, he never made any serious efforts to extricate himself from the entanglement.

LOSING EUROPE

For all its dangers hindsight remains a useful perspective for historians. It enables them to detect turning points and/or watersheds in careers and lives when the individual involved may simply have perceived only a temporary problem or advantage. Napoleon's involvement in Spain in 1808 is a good example of such a turning point. It did not seem especially significant at the time; moreover, the Napoleonic Empire continued to grow and did not reach its fullest territorial extent until 1810. But the war in Spain proved to be a war unlike any of those that Napoleon had fought before. There was to be no speedy, successful campaign that compelled the enemy to negotiate. Previously Napoleon had fought against monarchs who had tended to yield and sue for peace when heavily defeated on the battlefield; now he found himself engaged with a bewildering mixture of Spanish armies and ir-regulars, backed by a well-led, well-equipped, and well-supplied Anglo-Portuguese army. The Spanish war required more and more conscripts, and this fostered more and more resentment in France and elsewhere within the Empire. The First Consul had brought peace and security. The Emperor appeared to bring nothing but new wars and greater demands for men.

The war with Spain provided an opportunity for Napoleon's enemies. Britain exploited the situation from the outset. Early in 1809 the Austrians saw an opportunity for avenging Austerlitz, and in so doing they caught Napoleon off guard. The Austrian victory at Aspern-Essling (20–21 May 1809) destroyed the myth of French invincibility and sparked a series of small military uprisings in other German lands. The German uprisings were poorly supported. Napoleon was able to rescue the situation with a victory at Wagram (6 July) that forced the Austrians to request an armistice. He exacted harsh peace terms. Austria was required to cede territory to France, Bavaria and the Grand Duchy of Warsaw. She had to pay an indemnity, limit the size of her army and, of course, exclude all British products. This did nothing to assuage the Austrians' hostility towards Napoleon – nor did his taking of an Austrian bride, Marie-Louise, the favourite daughter of the Austrian Emperor Francis I.

The *senatus consultum* that had established the Empire had declared that

Napoleon's brothers would be his heirs. But it would have been surprising if a man of Napoleon's ambition and vanity had not wanted a son of his own to succeed. Josephine had not given him that son, or indeed any children of his own. He divorced her at the end of 1809, though she was allowed to keep the rank and title of empress. A teenage Austrian princess seemed the perfect bride. First, she brought added lustre to the Bonaparte family by linking them to the Habsburgs, one of the oldest dynasties in Europe. Second, she appeared likely to produce an heir, and dutifully did so in March 1811 just under a year after they were married. The child, a son named Napoleon, was proclaimed the King of Rome, a title previously given to the first son of the Holy Roman Emperor and thus enabling Napoleon to link his dynasty with the line running back to Charlemagne. However the marriage also had negative effects both within and outside France. Old French republicans recalled that Louis XVI, executed by revolutionaries in 1793, had also married a Habsburg princess, and she, Marie Antoinette, had been the aunt of the current Austrian emperor. Before the opportunity of marriage to Marie Louise had materialised, Napoleon had considered marrying the sister of Alexander of Russia. While Alexander had been lukewarm towards the idea, he still felt slighted by the marriage to Marie Louise. Alexander was also disappointed by the Peace of Schönbrunn that had ended the Wagram campaign. The Grand Duchy of Warsaw, which he had hoped to acquire, was now firmly established as a French satellite, and looked like being just one of several such that were being established in the Baltic region on Russia's border. In addition, nothing had come of promises made at Tilsit regarding a division of the Ottoman Empire and while the Continental Blockade might be providing some benefits for the French economy, it appeared to have had only serious adverse effects on that of Russia.

Relations with Russia did not improve during 1811. Some imperial notables and economic interests urged *rapprochement* or, at least, caution. Napoleon, however, appears to have relished the chance of war with Russia. There have been suggestions that the war with Russia was part of some plan for ultimately embarking on a grand campaign to India to take on the British there. But more prosaically, and much more likely, Napoleon wanted to bring another monarch to heel, as he had with Austria and Prussia, and to ensure that his Continental Blockade was solid. In June 1812, with a massive army and supremely confident of humbling the Tsar and his army, Napoleon crossed the Nieman and launched his disastrous Russian campaign. Moscow was entered on 14 September, but the Russian army, though severely bloodied at Borodino (7 September), simply withdrew and Alexander showed no intention of suing for an armistice. After a month, Napoleon ordered his army to evacuate Moscow and withdraw, thus beginning the terrible retreat during which the Grand Army was decimated by the ferocious combination of Russian weather, dwindling supplies and pin-prick attacks by Russian forces (*Doc. 16a*). On 5 December Napoleon left the army and hastened back to Paris. In his absence an attempted coup had illustrated that, even though he now had an heir to continue the dynasty together with an efficient and subservient administration, at its heart his Empire was not as secure as he had assumed. Indeed, one reason for the stress on Napoleon's health at the end of the 29th Bulletin of the Grand Army (*Doc. 16b*), issued as he left the army, was probably a desire to scotch the story of his death circulated by General Malet and his co-conspirators.

Claude-François de Malet had been born into the minor nobility but he had sided with the Revolution and risen to the rank of general. In 1804, as general commanding in the Department of the Charente, he had refused to authorise any celebrations following the plebiscite on Napoleon's imperial title. In 1807 he had been cashiered. In the following year he was involved in a conspiracy, was arrested and incarcerated first in a prison then in an asylum. In October 1812, with a small band of accomplices, he escaped from his asylum and, resplendent in his uniform he announced to the military in Paris that Napoleon had been killed in Russia and that the Republic was to be re-established (*Doc. 15*). Everyone fell in behind Malet unquestioningly, until the commander of the Paris garrison hesitated and then resisted. General Hulin was shot in the face for his pains, and the question remains as to what might have happened had Malet and his accomplices persevered with their bluff rather than shoot Hulin. Once the conspirators had shown their hand, however, the game was up; they were arrested, tried and shot. The ease with which Malet had threatened the Empire and the dynasty shook Napoleon. He was shocked, in particular, that no one had apparently thought of declaring a regency. The conspiracy contributed significantly to his decision to quit his army and return to Paris.

The military disaster in Russia encouraged the Prussian general Yorck, commanding a corps on the wing of the imperial army, to sign the Convention of Tauroggen (30 December 1812) with the advancing Russians promising to keep Yorck's men neutral. A second general, von Bülow, did not sign a convention, but allowed the Russians to advance across the territory that he was supposed to defend. Frederick William III remained fearful of a new war with Napoleon, but by mid-February 1813 two-thirds of his army was acting independently and out of his control. At the end of the month Prussia signed an alliance with Russia. The Austrians, wary of Russia and France signing another Tilsit treaty that would squeeze their interests, considered mediation, but then they also opted to join the new alliance. The states of the *Rheinbund*, who had been prepared to back Napoleon in their own interests, and especially against Austria and Prussia, now saw uniting against their 'Protector' as the best chance of preserving what they had gained over the previous decade. As ever, the British were on hand with the promise of subsidies and matériel.

LOSING FRANCE

The unravelling of Napoleon's Empire and alliances gathered momentum during 1813, reaching its climax in the massive battle of Leipzig (16–19 October). Over half a million men confronted each other in the 'Battle of the Nations' (*die Völkerschlacht*) and Napoleon, heavily outnumbered, was defeated and compelled to retreat. By the end of that year he had been forced back to the old frontiers of northern France, while south-western France was invaded by Wellington's army moving north from Spain. In the early months of 1814 Napoleon fought one of his most brilliant campaigns challenging and checking Austrian, Prussian, Russian and Swedish armies along the frontier of northern France with an imperial army that had more than the usual number of untried conscripts. But the odds were impossible. At the beginning of April a provisional government was established under Talleyrand, Napoleon's former foreign minister, and the Senate deposed Napoleon. Initially the Emperor tried to abdicate in favour of his infant son, but on 11 April he abdicated unconditionally and the Senate summoned the comte de Provence, brother of the executed Louis XVI and uncle of the disappeared Louis XVII, to accept the crown as Louis XVIII.

The victorious allies agreed that Napoleon should be allowed to keep his title of Emperor; his new 'empire' was the Mediterranean island of Elba, roughly 19 miles long and just over 6 miles wide. But Viscount Castlereagh and Prince Metternich, respectively the British and Austrian foreign ministers, did not consider Elba to be a particularly secure place to keep Napoleon. Once installed on the island Napoleon vigorously set about the administration of his new territory, but he was suspicious of the allied powers negotiating at the Congress of Vienna. Were Castlereagh and Metternich, not to mention the restored Bourbon monarchy in France, now planning to eject him from Elba, and his brother-in-law, Murat, from Naples? Murat – King Gioacchino Napoleone – was the last of the monarchs that he had created who still kept a throne. Napoleon was annoyed by the Bourbons' delay in paying the annuity they had promised him, and their refusal to answer his correspondence. His informants within France told him of disaffection in the army, of anger among people who found themselves dispossessed of property legally acquired during the Revolution, of dislike among many for the old-style pomp, ceremony and religiosity of the newly restored regime. At the beginning of 1815 he made his move. On 1 March, with a few hundred followers, he landed again in France and headed north for Paris. This final gamble is popularly known by the length of time that it lasted – a hundred days; while to keepers of the Napoleonic flame it remains 'the flight of the eagle'.

Fortified towns opened their gates to Napoleon and his small band of supporters, and the band grew in numbers as the old Emperor's charisma encouraged regiment after regiment to defect rather than fight him. On the night of 19–20 March Louis XVIII and his entourage left Paris. On 20 March 1815 Napoleon was installed, once again, in the Tuileries Palace. He probably intended, eventually, to pick up the reigns of power where he had left them, but the circumstances of France in the spring of 1815 compelled him to make liberal concessions and to draw support from social and political groups that he had previously largely ignored. Many feared that Louis XVIII would seek to restore the feudal authority of the old nobility and the old powers of the Church; while the very reappearance of Napoleon threatened invasion by the allied powers still deliberating at the Congress of Vienna. These twin fears brought a flurry of rhetoric reminiscent of the Jacobin Republic of 1793. Moreover, old Jacobins reappeared to play prominent roles in the spontaneous and heterogeneous *fédérés* movement that sprang up in different parts of France to support the liberal Emperor and to resist royalism, the clergy and invasion by the allied armies (Alexander, 1991). The Emperor himself, in his new liberal guise, approached liberal thinkers and politicians and persuaded one of their number, Benjamin Constant, to draft a supplementary document to the previous imperial constitutions. This *Acte Additionnel* promised, among other things, liberty of the press and the publication of parliamentary debates. It was published on 22 April and promptly submitted to a plebiscite. A majority supported the *Acte* – 1.55 million votes to a mere 5,740 – but the turnout was scarcely more than one in five of those eligible to vote, and in some areas, notably the north and especially the old royalist west and south and the cities of Bordeaux and Marseilles, the number of abstentions was massive. In some areas, it appears, the royalists were able to have a strong influence on the result, but probably many other men preferred to wait and see the outcome of the new war – and they did not have long to wait.

Napoleon would doubtless have preferred not to have to engage immediately in a war with his old enemies. Indeed, two weeks after his return to Paris he dispatched a circular letter to his 'brother' sovereigns declaring friendship (*Doc. 17*). But his 'brother' sovereigns would have none of it and mobilised their armies. On 11 June Napoleon left Paris to join his army on the Belgian border. A week later, after two indecisive clashes with allied forces at Ligny and Quatre Bras, he faced Wellington's motley allied army at Waterloo. Repeated French attacks failed to break Wellington's line, and the arrival of Blücher's Prussian army ensured Napoleon's defeat – and his second abdication. Blücher wanted Napoleon to be shot, preferably over the grave of the duc d'Enghien in the ditch at the fortress of Vincennes, but his British allies were rather more magnanimous. Napoleon surrendered to the captain of a British warship in early July. He appears to have harboured expectations that he might be able to live a private life, even in England, as a country gentleman. The British government, however, had no intention of letting him set foot in England, and no intention of situating him in any location from which he could easily launch another adventure on to French soil. On 15 October 1815 Napoleon and a small group of companions were landed on the British colony of St Helena – an island 1,100 miles from the nearest shores of West Africa. It was there that Napoleon was to spend the last years of his life, and it was there that he was to dictate memoirs that were to elaborate the earlier embroidery worked on his career, and vividly colour his legend.

MASTERING HISTORY

Napoleon had always been conscious of how best to portray himself and his achievements. He had a thirst for all forms of knowledge, and especially historical knowledge to which he turned time and again for examples, parallels and precedents to legitimise his regime and dynasty. In many respects he can be seen as a forerunner of modern authoritarian rulers who deploy all available forms of the media to project the best image of themselves and their regime, and to slant the representation of events in order to provide the best possible interpretation. Napoleon was by no means the first to do this; indeed, in many respects, he built on the manipulation of the arts that he had inherited from the French Revolution. But whereas the revolutionaries had sought to project a moral or political vision, Napoleon manipulated the arts and the media towards his personal glory. He drew on the late eighteenth-century fascination for neo-classical images, and he amplified this with emblems supposedly drawn from the old Kingdom of the Franks, thus linking himself with both imperial Rome and Charlemagne (Jourdan, 1996, 1998, 2000).

Artists were commissioned and prizes were offered for works celebrating key moments of his career. Historical accuracy was less important than the image presented in both paintings and sculptures. David, the great chronicler of revolutionary events, who was lucky to escape with his life when the Robespierrists were purged in 1794, resisted General Bonaparte's invitations until the inauguration of the Consulate. His reworking of the Pope's blessing in his coronation painting has already been noted; the same painting was similarly required to include Napoleon's mother and Cardinal Caprara, both of whom had disapproved of the event, and neither of whom had been present. David similarly depicted Napoleon distributing the eagle standards to his regiments. The event had taken place on 5 December 1804 and the initial painting showed the Emperor and his Empress; however, by the completion of the canvas, in 1810, Josephine had been divorced and, in consequence, she had to be discreetly painted out. Throughout the Consulate and Empire, David was working on his own, personal commission of the Spartan King Leonidas and his men waiting for the Persian invaders in the pass of Thermopylae. Napoleon intensely disliked this painting, given the outcome of the battle and the death of Leonidas and his 300 men; it did not suit with his personal hopes and expectations. While David increasingly fell from favour, other artists – including several of his pupils – thrived. Antoine-Jean Gros, for example, depicted the heroic General Bonaparte leading his men across the bridge at Arcola into the mouths of Austrian cannon (1796). His representation of Bonaparte visiting his men in the plague hospital at Jaffa during the disastrous Egyptian campaign (1804) showed the young general offering a healing touch to his stricken men, reminiscent of the miraculous cures believed to be in the hands of holy medieval monarchs, or even, as one contemporary critic has described it, 'a Christ-like general in Christ's own land' (Wilson-Smith, 1996: 160; and see Plate 2). Gros's picture of the bloody stalemate of Eylau was rather more ambiguous. Again Napoleon was presented in something of a Christ-like form, holding out his right hand in blessing while his enemies knelt in prayer at his side (see Plate 3). But the painting also focused on the suffering of the troops, arguably suiting well with a more sombre mood within France resulting from continuing wars and lengthening casualty lists. Most important at the time, however, was that Napoleon liked it and, in consequence, the painting received official approval, won the prize for which it was submitted, and Gros got the *Légion d'honneur* (Prendergast, 1997).

Painting is, perhaps, the most obvious visual medium of the period; but Napoleon also embarked on a significant programme of rebuilding and public works in Paris. Much of this work was responding to problems that had existed for some time; but some of his attempts to improve the provisioning of the capital also stemmed from concerns about the popular unrest occasioned by food shortages, especially in the aftermath of the Revolution. The new east–west axis of the rue de Rivoli was begun; new abattoirs and markets were built; and the fresh water supply was improved by the cutting of the Ourcq canal and the construction of new fountains – all of which enabled some further celebration of Napoleon and his career. Rivoli was one of his greatest Italian triumphs, and running out of the new road were, and still are, the rue Castiglione and the rue des Pyramides. New buildings and new fountains were expected to carry bas-reliefs or carvings of his career or of important events or characters from French history. Other works had less practical ends, but were designed to promote architecture and to beautify Paris, making it appear to be the supreme capital of Europe. There was also much stress on the origins of this supremacy with the arc du Carrousel, the arc de Triomphe, the Vendôme Column, and the architectural competition to rebuild the old Church of La Madeleine as the Temple of Glory.

The visual representation of himself and his regime was important to

Napoleon, but so too was the written representation. He regretted that writers seemed to do so little for the regime, but he had imposed censorship on the press and had strictly limited the number of media outlets. One of the earliest decrees of the Consulate reduced the number of daily newspapers in Paris from 73 to 13, and within a decade the number had been reduced still further to just four, all of which were required to publish only information acceptable to, and often largely received from, the government. The press in the provincial departments was similarly reduced and restricted; a decree of August 1810 limited the number of newpapers to one in each department. From 1811 the best-known of the Paris journals, *Le Moniteur*, had all of its political articles edited by Hughes-Bernard Maret, one of Napoleon's most trusted ministers. Among the key documents included in *Le Moniteur* – which were also specially printed for distribution and public exhibition across the Empire – were the periodic bulletins of the *Grande Armée* which glorified victories and played down defeats. These bulletins, designed to inspire confidence in the Emperor and his army, were written by Napoleon himself. The first appeared during the Austerlitz campaign; but perhaps the most notorious bulletin was the 29th, written at the end of the Russian campaign of 1812. While this bulletin made some reference to the disaster that had overtaken the army, it endeavoured to lighten the defeat by stressing that the Emperor himself remained fit and capable (*Doc. 16b*, and see above p. 22). A saying then became common throughout the army, *menteur comme un bulletin* (false like a bulletin), and a *Bulletin* itself was often termed a *Menteur* (liar). This probably reflected the cynical humour of the soldiery rather than any serious hostility to the Emperor and his regime. Moreover, as Alan Forrest has pointed out, the *Bulletins* were also read with enthusiasm. They said what soldiers and others probably wanted to believe – that one last effort would bring ultimate victory, and that Napoleon would bring them through. Unlike the abstract principles that characterised the Revolution's declarations, Napoleon's *Bulletins* possessed a personal and immediate quality; the cause was one shared between the Emperor and his men, his glory was also their glory. They loved him for it, and would follow him anywhere (*Doc. 9*; Forrest, 2002: 71–5).

The enforced exile on St Helena gave Napoleon long days with nothing much to do other than reflect upon his triumphs and misfortunes. It is unlikely that he was not conscious of reworking the events of his life to put the best gloss upon them, though it is also possible that egoism led him to believe much of what he said. Annie Jourdan has noted his concerns that those who had triumphed over him would be able to produce their view of events with scant regard for truth; 'by the time of the exile of St. Helena Napoleon was aware that the memory of him would depend on the testimony he left behind: thus he was prepared to distort the facts' (Jourdan, 1996: 342).

There is no shape to the memoirs that were written on St Helena, and certainly no chronological analysis of his career. The memoirs were dictated, and since the most celebrated of his memorialists, the comte de Las Cases, was ejected from the island in November 1816 for criticism of the governor, there was no opportunity for Napoleon to correct and rework them, even had he so wished. The memoirs show a profound awareness of the problems of analysing historical sources and of subsequently writing a historical narrative; but they also reveal a cynicism about the writing of history (*Doc. 18a*). They portray Napoleon as having altruistic ambition and acting always in the best interests of France (*Doc. 18b*). They describe him as resolving the chaos of the Revolution, eager for peace and security, but always thwarted by the envious, established crowned heads of Europe and, above all, by the money-grubbing, jealous English (*Doc. 18c*). The story is given a novel human quality by the way that Las Cases interwove Napoleon's words with the day-to-day confrontations that he blamed on Sir Hudson Lowe, the British governor of the island, who is portrayed throughout as petty and mean-spirited. From its first publication in France in 1823 Las Cases's *Mémorial de St. Hélène* has provided Napoleon's apologists with a more or less official interpretation of events, and more critical historians with a range of argument and statements to debate and evaluate.

UNDERSTANDING THE MAN

What Napoleon lacked in modesty he more than made up for in ambition and self-confidence. Moreover, he was extremely hard working and able. On campaign in the early years of his career he often scarcely slept. When in Paris he was known regularly to work through much of the night, going to bed at 10.00 p.m., rising at 2.00 a.m. and working till 5.00 a.m., then returning to bed until 7.00 a.m. His days in Paris were then filled with meetings, reading and correcting documents and receiving petitions, with food being eaten while he was standing or on the move (see Plate 4). His insatiable thirst for, and ability to absorb, knowledge enabled him to discuss science with scientists, and to debate, at a high level and with experts, history, geography, literature and the cultural traditions and aspirations of different states and different nations. He expected regular reports from his subordinates, and he read them. He wrote an enormous number of letters and directives, variously estimated at between 54,000 and 70,000 in the 15 years of his rule. In one week, shortly after becoming Viceroy of Italy, Eugène de Beauharnais received 21 letters providing advice and instructions, some of them running to several pages (see, for example, *Doc. 11a*).

Napoleon could be fortunate on the battlefield, as at Marengo, but he also conducted brilliant campaigns such as that on the French frontier in 1814 when his army contained thousands of raw troops. He could be overbearing or devious in diplomacy, but so too could his opponents; it is clear, for instance, that Metternich deliberately used the opportunity of the Peace of Schönbrunn of 1809 to aggravate the gulf emerging between Napoleon and Tsar Alexander. He was calm and level headed in battle and at court, but he could also flare into ferocious rages, flinging verbal abuse at his subordinates and sometimes lashing out at servants or soldiers with fists, feet or riding crop; even the unfortunate Pius VII was reported to have been pushed around during one of his more tense encounters with Napoleon. At times, too, Napoleon could be brutal and ruthless, even to the point of folly as with the kidnapping and execution of the duc d'Enghien in 1804. But then no one could have scrambled to the top in the wake of the French Revolution and won plaudits for bringing order and security by turning the other cheek. He carefully manipulated his image, but he undoubtedly had charisma and men turned to him and followed him. Marshal Ney was probably sincere in promising to arrest Napoleon on the latter's return from Elba; but, instead, he rallied to him. It is a vexing question, but one that biographers invariably feel that they have to address: what motivated this man? Was it pure egotism, pure ambition, larded with some very good luck? And can this egotism and ambition be best explained by nature, or nurture, or what?

There have been attempts to put Napoleon on the psychiatrist's couch and – from an analysis of his behaviour, his own writings and those of others – to understand his personality. His behaviour has been put down to a Corsican 'primitivity' which made him impatient with the abstract and a believer in the idea that human problems could be solved by force. It has been suggested that he was driven by a latent homosexuality (Richardson, 1972). His isolation at military school, aggravated by the death of his father during that period, has been seen as influential in his development. But it has also been stressed that he was ambivalent towards his father: he never acknowledged that he owed his education to his father's efforts, and criticised him as much, or even more, than he praised him. He has been said to have had a complex about his elder brother Joseph, first yearning to supplant him and then indulging him. His mother, Letizia – *Madame mère* as she was known, using the term reserved for dowager queens under the old regime – is commonly seen to have had an enormous impact on him. She left him, according to one biographer, with 'an unconscious desire for revenge against the opposite sex. ... In particular, he always thought of women as being totally without honour, duplicitous, deceivers, liars' (McLynn, 1997: 13). The relationship with Josephine is also sometimes deployed as a symptom and an explanation of his behaviour. Before they married she was the widow of a general guillotined two years earlier; she was older, with two children by her first marriage, and some contemporary comment cruelly suggested that her beauty was fading fast. Yet it does not appear that this was a political marriage arranged to relieve Barras of a mistress and to ensure that Bonaparte got command of the army of Italy. He was stung by Josephine's infidelities, reported to him during the Egyptian campaign. However, in spite of his many dalliances with other women, she was the only woman with whom he sought a lasting emotional relationship. It has been suggested that, initially, Bonaparte saw her as a younger version of his mother, and thus a woman that he sought to impress with his first notable military campaign in Italy. The infidelities on both sides subsequently numbed his ability to form intimate human relationships, but fostered his ability to command and dominate (Parker, 1971). He nevertheless appears to have enjoyed a long relationship with the Polish countess Marie Waleska that was both intimate and human. Freudian explanations are not to every historian's taste, and an Oedipal complex is probably not necessary to explain pronounced egotism and ambition.

Whether the historian opts for this form of psychoanalytical history or not, in the end he or she is left with the fact that Napoleon was convinced of his abilities to defeat enemies both on the battlefield and at the conference table. For most of his career this self-belief worked. Indeed, success after success seems to have convinced Napoleon of his great destiny. 'All my life', he wrote to Josephine in 1807, 'I have sacrificed everything – comfort, self-interest, happiness – to my destiny' (quoted in Herold, 1955: 40). 'Destiny' was a concept that recurred in his writings and reminiscences. Moreover, with no significant opposition or check to his personal power, and with artists and courtiers prepared to portray him as he wished and, generally, to give him such answers as he wished, it is hardly surprising that he developed feelings of infallibility. It is easy for the historian with hindsight to see that the involvement in Spain and the invasion of Russia were acts of folly, but in 1808 there was no reason to suppose that a war in Spain would develop as it did; and in 1812 there was no reason to suppose that the Tsar would simply withdraw from Moscow and refuse any form of negotiation. Other enemies had not behaved in such fashions.

Napoleon's phenomenal energy and application to work enabled him to direct his military campaigns and, at the same time, to consider the internal reorganisation of France, his Empire and his satellite states. Yet there is a further conundrum: his abilities, at times, appear to have been clouded by his determination to plant members of his family as the rulers of reorganised kingdoms. It is difficult to know how to explain all of this. According to Louis Bergeron: '[a]s for his own family, he felt as a Corsican the sentiments of solidarity and "the duties of the son who has succeeded" ' (Bergeron, 1981: 13–14). Bergeron, however, also notes that Napoleon's family often responded to his largesse with jealousy and pettiness. Was it simply Corsican clannishness and the tradition of putting the family first that led to the elevation of other Bonapartes? Corsicans appear to have stuck together, but they also engaged in vicious feuds and the clashes with Paoli in 1792–93 contain elements of Corsican factionalism. Saliceti, the Corsican deputy keen to maintain links with the Jacobin-dominated Convention, was responsible for ensuring that Captain Bonaparte got command of the artillery at Toulon. Corsicans, however, were not alone in this, and some French people who were known to a young French officer could be vitally important for a military promotion even during the Revolution; Barras, after all, was no Corsican. The questions must remain open as to whether Napoleon continued to hold some vestiges of Corsican ideas about putting family first, or whether he believed that members of his family shared his abilities. Was he, perhaps, reluctant to trust others outside the family more than was absolutely necessary? It must also be remembered that it was usual for other royal houses in Europe to marry off members of the family in order to cement alliances; how else did Napoleon secure a Habsburg bride? Napoleon's family members were given friendly advice on how to run their kingdoms, but they were never allowed to forget who was responsible for their elevation and were brutally reprimanded for errors and shortcomings (*Docs. 11a–d and 12*). When, for example, Murat followed Napoleon's lead and left the army retreating from Russia, he was bluntly told: 'The title of King has turned your head: if you want to keep it, behave yourself, and be careful what you say' (quoted in Thompson, 1998: 279). Similarly, any member of the family who became too popular with his new subjects could run into trouble. As King of Holland, Louis Bonaparte took the situation of his subjects seriously and began to win popular support. Napoleon had little time for this and was highly critical of the feeble Dutch implementation of his Continental Blockade and of their response to the British expedition to Walcheren Island in the Scheldt during the late summer of 1809. The following year Louis considered defending Amsterdam against his brother, but in the end he accepted a forced abdication and saw the whole of his kingdom annexed to France.

The facts of Napoleon's career are indeed clear; understanding the man and his motives remains difficult. It is now necessary, however, to switch the angle of investigation from the man, his personality and motives, to the changes that were wrought in France under his direction.

CHAPTER THREE

REORGANISING FRANCE

Napoleon brought internal stability to France after the upheaval of the Revolution. He fostered reconciliation between old and new élites and restored the Catholic Church – on his own terms. The 15 years of Napoleon's rule witnessed significant reorganisation within France: central and local government were restructured, new legal codes were promulgated, and education was reformed. Many of these changes are increasingly seen by historians as a climax to a programme of reforms advocated during the Enlightenment, begun during the Revolution, and finally cemented in place when the Bourbons were restored after Napoleon's fall. Even so, it would be wrong to think in terms of a simple linear development. While some reforms that began under the Revolution were continued under Napoleon, it was sometimes in a considerably modified form, and some Revolutionary ideas were simply abandoned by a regime that was, in many respects, very traditional in its outlook (Woloch, 1994, 2001b).

FOUNDATIONS

No regime can exist without support. Napoleon sought to base his regime on what he termed *les masses de granit* – literally 'the masses of granite', the *notables* of France. From the beginning of the Consulate he wanted to know who were the most important men in local society, and by important he meant those who paid the most in property tax. A survey was initiated into the top 600 taxpayers in each department, and this was extended with subsequent requests for detailed information on those at the top of the list. These were the men who, Napoleon believed, could ensure stability through influencing other members of society by their words, their behaviour and the use of their money. The regime's surveys of the *notables*, and particularly the membership lists of the electoral colleges compiled in 1810, have provided historians with the opportunity of constructing a profile of the élite of Napoleonic France (see Table 1).

Table 1 Known occupations of the *notables* in 1810

Occupation	Percentage
Landed proprietors (*propriétaires*)	24.6
Local administrators	18.1
State functionaries	15.8
Liberal professions	14.4
Commerce/industry	10.8
Owner-occupiers (*propriétaires-exploitants*)	8.2
Military officers	2.3
Clergy	1.2
Others	4.6

Source: Based on Bergeron, Louis, *France Under Napoleon*, translated by R.R. Palmer, p. 69. Copyright © 1981 by Princeton University Press. Reprinted by permission of Princeton University Press.

As can be seen from Table 1, there were four principal kinds of men making up the *notables*: landowners, administrators, professional men and businessmen. However, it is not always easy clearly to differentiate between them. Both professional men and businessmen continued to associate the productive use of money with the acquisition of land. Consequently men who had become wealthy from business often sought to buy land since it was as a landowner, not as the possessor of movable wealth, that a man was deemed to have reached the top of the social scale. The Revolution had swept away power that depended on birth and inherited rank but many of the landowners among the *notables* had, under successive Revolutionary governments, profited from the sale of *biens nationaux*, namely that property confiscated by the State from the Church and from *émigrés*. There were wide local variations in degrees of wealth among them. There were also varieties in social origin. Some came from the old regime nobility; they had kept their heads down during the upheavals of the 1790s, or subsequently rallied to the regime. Others had relatively new money. The great majority of these landowners, or their fathers, had been in possession of some property at the outset of the Revolution; and the Revolution had given them the opportunity to enlarge that property. Napoleon ensured that they would keep their gains through clauses in the Concordat and the Civil Code that ensured full legal title to lands acquired from the Church or from *émigrés* during the Revolution. But having given them security of their land, he wanted their political loyalty, and without yielding to them any real political power.

By the 'Constitution of the Year X' (the *senatus consultum* of 4 August 1802) the filtering of the electoral process (see above, p. 13) was narrowed still further. Henceforth the 200 to 300 members of a departmental electoral college could only be appointed from the 600 leading taxpayers in each department, and the First Consul himself was able to nominate up to ten members from among the 30 highest taxpayers. Membership of the electoral college gave the *notables* additional prestige rather than political power, but there were also opportunities for them to play administrative roles and formally to exert authority within the State's structure.

Some landed proprietors took on the lower administrative posts and duties in their districts. But Napoleon never intended that the men of property should take over the administration of the State simply because of their wealth and social standing; like the men of 1789 he wanted a meritocratic hierarchy. Under the Consulate he had to rely on men who had honed their bureaucratic abilities at the close of the old regime or during the Revolution; roughly 40 percent of his first appointments to the post of departmental prefect were revolutionaries who had served in at least one of the legislative assemblies established during the revolutionary decade. At the same time he also set about developing a new administrative élite that was to have its foundations in service, that would be perpetuated by wealth received as a reward for that service, and that would be loyal to his regime. He looked to the sons of the *notables* and of others slightly lower on the social scale for this élite. The corps of *auditeurs* of the *Conseil d'État* eventually numbered 400 men and was first established in 1803. It was only open to a few, but it provides the best example of Napoleon's aspirations in this respect. The *auditeurs* were young men from élite families who were expected to have no nostalgic feelings for either the old regime or the Revolution, and who were recruited initially to provide assistance to the council and the ministries. The post was the first rung on the ladder to top jobs within the bureaucracy. From here the *auditeurs* moved to junior posts in the administration both in France and across the Empire. The climax to this stage of their career was appointment to one of the key positions such as that of a prefect, and from here they could aspire to move on to run a ministry in Paris. *Auditeurs* had to have satisfied the conscription laws, though this did not necessarily mean having served in the army in person. They had to have a minimum income of 6,000 francs a year and, after 1812, they had also to have a university degree in law or science (*Doc. 10*). As the regime progressed, the number of professional administrators running the Empire who had begun their career as *auditeurs* and had risen steadily through the hierarchy, became more and more marked. This meant that the core of the administration was gradually becoming younger. At the same time, however, the number of men who could trace their lineage to the nobility of the old regime also became more marked (Whitcomb, 1974, 1979).

Perhaps what is most surprising in the list of the *notables* is the relatively small number of military men. Nevertheless military values were highly regarded and greatly rewarded by Napoleon. The army was another

Table 2   Origins of imperial nobility

Occupation	Percentage
Military	59
Senior State functionary	22
Other *notable*	17
Others (commerce, etc.)	2

Source: Adapted from Bergeron. Copyright © Princeton University Press.

route for the sons of *notables*, and for others, to achieve honour, prestige and wealth. Towards the end of the Empire, of the 32,000 members of the *Légion d'honneur* only some 1,500 were civilians, and membership of the *Légion* brought an annual salary. The military also figured significantly in the new Napoleonic nobility established in 1808 (see Table 2).

At the top of the hierarchy of the imperial nobility were members of the Bonaparte family and the military marshals. Particularly interesting here, however, was the fact that 22.5 percent of those ennobled by Napoleon came from families that had been noble under the old regime. As well as seeking to reward men from the old Third Estate who supported him and who, in some instances, were discomforted by their new titles, Napoleon also used the imperial nobility to cement the support of old regime nobles who had rallied to him. The new nobility, however, was not to be like its predecessor, and the word 'nobility' was not formally employed to describe it. The new, imperial nobility was much smaller, perhaps only one-seventh of the size its predecessor had been in 1789. Moreover, the titles were personal and could only be handed down to an heir if there was a guaranteed level of wealth to preserve the dignity of the rank. The level of wealth varied according to rank and had to be verified by the Council of the Seal of Titles. In some instances Napoleon went so far as to provide the assets necessary for the *majorat* or entail. The key point is that the titles of the new nobility were linked directly to public service; all bishops – by the Concordat the clergy became confirmed as State servants – all prefects, and all similar high State officials, thus acquired at least the rank of baron.

Napoleon's regime followed an active policy of seeking to secure support from both survivors of the old nobility and men of the Revolution. The words *amalgame* and *ralliement* were used at the time. The former implied the end of the social divisions of the old regime, the reconciliation of old political enemies, and a fusion of members of the old nobility and former revolutionaries into a new ruling élite. *Ralliement* meant, literally, members of the old nobility and former Jacobins rallying round the new regime. Historians continue to argue about the extent to which the words reflect any reality during the period. The problem is compounded by regional variations and by the personalities and situations of different individuals and groups of individuals. Two examples from the department of Mayenne offer a flavour of the complexities and responses among the old nobility. The family of Henri-Alexis Breon de Lancrau had been resident in Marigné-Peuton for generations. Henri-Alexis had been an officer in the old regime army who subsequently fought in the *émigré* armies against the Revolution. By 1806, however, he was back in France and was appointed mayor of Marigné-Peuton. His advancement, albeit confined to his small, native community, may have been linked to the fact that his younger brother had married a protegée of Hortense de Beauharnais, Napoleon's step-daughter and wife to Louis, King of Holland. Even so, the sub-prefect of Chateau-Gontier could report that he had heard nothing but good of Henri-Alexis who spent his time, with his wife, pursuing agricultural projects and rebuilding part of their house. However, when Louis XVIII returned, Henri-Alexis rapidly declared for the Bourbons and even followed Louis into exile to Ghent during the Hundred Days. Etienne-Thomas Dean's family had been linked with Chateau-Gontier since the fifteenth century and had been ennobled in the seventeenth. The Deans suffered severely in the Revolution. Etienne-Thomas and his brother, both army officers, emigrated and fought with the *émigré* armies. Their mother and eldest sister were killed in 1794; their brother-in-law was killed fighting with the *Chouans* in 1800 – the same year that they returned to France and rallied to the new regime. In 1804 Etienne-Thomas put his signature to an address to the First Consul expressing 'the wish to see him seated on the throne of Charlemagne wearing the imperial crown, to see this as hereditary for his august family, in order to assure for ever the good fortune of all the French people'. In 1808 Etienne-Thomas became Mayor of Chateau-Gontier, a post from which, for health reasons, he resigned at the beginning of the Hundred Days. During the Restoration he became a royalist deputy for Mayenne.

Alongside these old nobles have to be contrasted the notables who owed much of their fortune to the Revolution and who also rallied to the imperial regime. In Mayenne, for example, Constant Paillard-Duclere was born into a bourgeois family in Laval and began life as a notary. He appears to have made a fortune from the sale of *biens nationaux* and became the proprietor of the biggest ironworks in the west of France employing 369 men in his forges at the end of the Empire. He served as mayor of Olivet from 1808 until 1824, and then, like Etienne-Thomas, he became a parliamentary deputy for Mayenne during the Restoration. Paillard-Duclere does not appear to have been an active revolutionary. Honoré-Landoald Aubert, in contrast, had been politically active in the Gironde. The son of a Parisian *marchand limonadier* he began his working life as a seigneurial agent. He acquired his own land, sided with the Girondin faction and, on their defeat, was fortunate to survive the Montagnard prescription. On the fall of Robespierre he re-emerged and held a succession of local administrative posts. These culminated in his appointment in 1801 as a subprefect in the department of the Gironde. In 1808 he was elected to the Legislative Body and received the *légion d'honneur* in 1814.

No matter how hard some prefects may have tried, it could be impossible to break the antagonism between returned *emigrés* and those men who had legally acquired their lands in their absence. The idea of *ralliement* thus had internal contradictions, and it also varied with shifts in the political and international situation. More of the old nobility appear to have become *ralliés* in the later, more conservative years of the Empire. But was this *ralliement* the result of the shifting policies of the regime, or because it appeared increasingly secure and successful? Did some members of the old nobility accept positions within the imperial State out of loyalty to the Emperor or more out of a long-established tradition of public duty? (Compare Bergeron, 1981: 125–33; Ellis, 1983; Tulard, 1984: 246–53.) Did some rally because of the opportunity – alien perhaps to modern thinking – for glory? Maurice de Roquemaurel was an old regime officer who fought in the *émigré* armies. But he returned to France in 1800 apparently through a desire to serve his native country, and enlisted as a simple trooper in a hussar regiment. By the Peace of Lunéville his abilities had seen him promoted to sub-lieutenant, but he yielded to his father's demands to return to his native Ariège, marry and ensure the perpetuation of the family line. His family duty done, in 1808 he was back in uniform and over the next few years he conducted a ferocious and successful campaign against Catalan irregulars and Spanish troops just across the border from his native department.

In the end the masses of granite turned out to be foundations of sand. As a group the *notables* were prepared to support Napoleon for as long as it remained in their interest, and, indeed, some of the soldiers behaved similarly. Nor was the mass of the population any different. The peace of 1801 brought the First Consul popularity, but the continuing demands of war, particularly the demands for conscription that increased considerably with the Russian campaign and its desperate aftermath, appear to have fostered weariness among most and a simmering resentment among many.

FINANCES AND THE ECONOMY

In many respects Napoleon proved to be a safe pair of hands, but he was conservative in economic matters, and while his imperial policy was effective for some areas of the economy in the short term, in the long run it created almost as many difficulties as it resolved.

Poor financial management had been a key element in precipitating the Revolution and bringing down the monarchy. The revolutionary decade with its disastrous experiments with paper money, its wars and its coups, did little to improve matters. The Directory initiated some reforms, but without significant effect. As First Consul, General Bonaparte recognised that bringing stability to French finances would secure his position and, with his customary ruthlessness and vigour, he promptly set out to establish a stable currency. Bad paper currency was eliminated by refusing to pay for supplies bought on credit, refusing to honour certain bonds, and declaring that specie was to be the only legal tender. On 16 *Nivôse* Year VIII (6 January 1800) the Bank of France was established with capital of 30 million francs divided into shares of 1,000 francs each. The 200 largest shareholders of the bank were to elect the 15 governors and three directors to run the bank – a move guaranteed to tie the country's financial élite to the new institution. The intention was that the new institution would provide credit to both the State and to entrepreneurs who regularly complained about the difficulty of negotiating loans.

For all his boldness in diplomacy and war, Napoleon was wary of an imaginative fiscal policy and a sophisticated use of credit. He always maintained that such policies would be Britain's downfall. Initially his measures achieved success in re-establishing financial confidence and in balancing the budget by 1802. But he looked to the financial system primarily for what it would yield in the short term, and to this end he ensured that it was effectively and rigorously managed at the points of both collection and distribution. Tax collectors and inspectors – who were paid in proportion to the taxes they collected – were appointed at departmental level. The tax receipts were passed up through receivers, who were required to post security bonds and were subject to inspection by Treasury officials. The Treasury itself required certified authorization for the release of any monies as well as detailed accounts from other ministries. The *Cour des comptes* was established in 1807 as a central bureau for auditing the State's finances.

The taxation system depended heavily on direct impositions on real estate and personal property. The land tax (*la contribution foncière*) was originally an assessment based on agricultural income. Napoleon hoped to establish a more equitable system based on the precise nature of land holding and, to this end, in 1807 he launched a new land register (*cadastre*) to measure and value landed property, and thus recalculate the land tax across the whole of France. This was to prove a massive task that was not to be completed until 1880; nevertheless, by the time Napoleon's Empire collapsed, just over one-fifth of the country had been assessed. Taxes on personal property (*la contribution personnelle mobilière*) fell more on towns people for their servants, horses, carriages and so on. This tax was progressively replaced by the *octroi*, a levy which, from September 1803, the larger municipalities could levy on consumer goods entering their towns.

The problem for the improved fiscal system was that State expenditure, and especially the cost of imperial adventures, steadily mounted from around 700 million francs in 1806 to over 1,000 million six years later. The demands of the military increased from 60 to 80 percent of the total, and the revenue collected increasingly fell short. In attempts to meet the deficits direct taxation was augmented by indirect taxes (*droits réunis*) on commodities such as alcoholic drinks, playing cards, salt and tobacco. Finally, in addition to these taxes, and to the receipts raised from customs duties and various registration and service charges, the imperial government also sought to profit from its military adventures and the expanding territories of the Empire. Various estimates have concluded, for example, that between 470 and 517 million francs were extracted from Prussia in the years 1806 to 1812. Even so, after the initial fiscal success of the Consulate, and in spite of the improved financial administration, the regime increasingly failed to cover its expenses.

Napoleon's fiscal policy was not greatly different from that of his predecessors, both royal and revolutionary. His achievement was to give it a solid basis, to make it work effectively and to provide it with an administrative structure that was to continue long after his fall. The new monetary standard based on a metallic currency, and finally established in March 1803, was to last for 125 years. But Napoleon cannot be said to have had any similar impact on the French economy. Again, he looked upon the economy for what it yielded of direct and immediate use to his regime.

Agriculture was the largest sector of the French economy and landownership, as was noted earlier, continued to be seen as important for social prestige. It is extremely difficult to detect significant change in the agricultural sector during the relatively short interval of the Consulate and Empire. This is partly because such change tends to occur over much longer periods, but also because of considerable regional variations. The complexities and regional differences have, in turn, engendered disagreements between historians. There was some cash cropping, and some medium-sized properties appear to have been well exploited by their owner-occupiers. But there were also thousands of labourers owning small plots insufficient for even their own needs. They clung to their property, and the inheritance law established in the Civil Code that gave all children the right to a share in their father's property perpetuated a system that militated against agricultural improvement on small, peasant-owned plots. Then there were tenants who were often reluctant to make improvements and investments, fearing that this would encourage an increase in their rent.

From their creation the departmental prefects were asked to report on the state of agricultural production within their jurisdictions. Complete statistics survive for the years 1810 to 1813. These were massaged by the comte de Montalivet, the Minister of the Interior, in a report of 1813 that demonstrated a thriving agricultural sector and prospering rural dwellers. Six years later the same figures were used in a rather different way by one of Montalivet's predecessors, Jean Chaptal, but also to demonstrate success.

Chaptal appears to have assumed that overall institutional changes were beneficial and so, in consequence, there must have been agricultural improvement. Grain prices rose during the period, which is probably indicative of a pressure on supply. There were poor harvests during the Consulate, followed by generally good ones except in the years 1806 and 1809–11. People often managed in the bad years by eating cereals usually used for livestock feed. In some areas there was a move to potato production, though this crop was also popularly considered as animal feed. There appears to have been little improvement in animal husbandry. Wine production was the one area of the sector that can be said to have prospered significantly during the Consulate and Empire (Le Goff and Sutherland, 1991).

Again utility was Napoleon's watchword and he hoped to be able to encourage industrial crops to substitute for colonial goods that could only be acquired in some way through arrangement or trade with the British. The Minister of the Interior decreed how much land in a department was to be handed over for such crops and the prefects allotted it. Such goods were coffee, cotton, dyes, tobacco and, most notably, cane sugar. In 1811 Napoleon set out to encourage the production of sugar beet and from 1 January 1813 the import of sugar cane, a trade dominated by the British as a result of their supremacy in the West Indies, was prohibited. The area given over to the production of beet did not meet the targets set; nevertheless the refining of beet sugar was to become one of the principal agricultural industries of nineteenth- and twentieth-century France.

Napoleon's wars and economic policies combined to develop a double shift in French trade that was already in motion by the time of the Revolution. First, French trade was shifting its focus away from the Atlantic and towards continental Europe and, second, it was becoming less centred on coffee, sugar and tobacco and more on cotton, coal and iron. The success of Britain's Royal Navy during the Revolutionary wars had blighted the fortunes of those merchants engaged in Atlantic trade. Their hopes that the Peace of Amiens would revive these fortunes were dashed by the resumption of war. The two Channel ports of Le Havre and Rouen were particularly badly hit since the Royal Navy's blockade was much tighter along the Channel sea lanes than around Bordeaux where the pressures were less acute and where neutral shipping, primarily American, was still active. The introduction of the Continental Blockade in 1806 checked Bordeaux's relative advantage (Crouzet, 1964; Butel, 1991; Daly, 2001).

Napoleon's Continental Blockade was formally introduced by his Berlin Decree of 21 November 1806 and strengthened by the Milan Decrees of 23 November and 17 December 1807 (*Doc. 13*). It had two interlinked aims. First, Napoleon wanted to eliminate Britain's capacity for military involvement on continental Europe. British naval supremacy following Trafalgar rendered naval conflict and invasion impossible in the short term. But French military dominance on continental Europe suggested that it would be possible to close off Britain's European markets, thus undermining her financially and forcing her to sue for peace. The logic of the blockade was that, if Britain failed to sell her goods in Europe she would build up a serious commercial and industrial surplus, be forced to use her bullion reserves to pay for necessary imports, and suffer major inflation. Second, Napoleon wanted to fill the gap left by the exclusion of British goods from Europe by building up and promoting French industry, trade and technology. This, he expected, would replace the losses accrued from the problems in the Atlantic trade. Moreover, the success of the French economy in Europe and the defeat of Britain could, ultimately, bring about a restoration of France's Atlantic trade. The first aim failed; the second had mixed results.

The blockade did nothing for the suffering seaports. But other sectors of the French economy prospered, not just from the exclusion of British goods but from imperial policies that gave advantages to French goods. Napoleon's Europe was never intended to be a common market, and this policy is apparent from the moment he came to power. The trade treaties that followed his alliances were usually designed to work to the benefit of France rather than her allies or dependants. Sometimes the favour to French industry could even be found at the heart of the Empire as when, for example, under the Consulate, the silk industry in the Piedmontese departments was undermined for the sake of that in Lyons (*Doc. 12*). Much of Italy became a reserved market (*marché réservé*) providing French industry with cheap raw materials, and compelled to buy certain products only from France. The Kingdom of Italy, for example, had its silk manufacturing industry virtually destroyed, though not its production of raw silk which was sent to France for manufacture. It was also required to purchase cotton goods from France and to turn its back on its traditional suppliers elsewhere in the peninsula and in Switzerland. Such policies helped the weakened cotton industry in Rouen, and contributed significantly to the prosperity of other cotton manufacturing districts, notably Lille, Mulhouse, Paris and, as a result of Belgium's incorporation into France, Ghent. In 1806 the region around Rouen had been the principal cotton manufacturing area of France; six years later the area around Lille produced nearly five times as much as that around Rouen. Mulhouse was also booming, not least because of two opportunities that it was able to exploit: the exclusive entry point for raw Levantine cotton was its fellow Alsatian town of Strasbourg; and its merchants had traditional links with nearby German and Swiss markets. Strasbourg itself, situated on the great waterway of the Rhine, became the major imperial *entrepôt* for the export of French textiles and wines to the Confederation of the Rhine and to territories further afield. It was a major entry point for permitted goods, both raw materials and finished articles;

and its merchants also profited from trade that passed along the Rhine between the Low Countries, Switzerland and Italy (Ellis, 1981; Daly, 2001).

French manufacturers never profited to the extent that Napoleon wished from the advantages he gave them. In what Stuart Woolf has called 'a remarkable admission of inferiority' the manufacturers of the department of Roër begged their prefect to keep textiles produced in the Grand Duchy of Berg out of their protected French and Italian markets.

> We conclude that: (1) our labour costs must be higher than on the right bank of the Rhine, as our labourers work less and spend more than those of Berg; (2) our goods are of a lower quality than those manufactured in the grand-duchy because, since our workers no longer find subsistence in the convents, they only work out of necessity, whereas the Berg workers strive to make their products as perfect as possible; (3) as a result, our factories could not withstand the competition of those of the grand-duchy of Berg, if it were annexed to the French empire. (Quoted in Woolf, 1991: 147)

Nor was it possible to keep out of France the cheap products of British industry and the colonial produce brought from British colonies, let alone keep these out of the rest of the Empire and its allies. Smuggling thrived, even though the number of customs officials was almost tripled from 12,000 in 1797 to more than 35,000 in 1810. Customs officials themselves, together with soldiers, policemen and other imperial functionaries, were tempted by the profits that could be made from illicit trade. Such trade involved both smuggling (*contrabande*), the trade in prohibited goods, and *fraude*, the trafficking in permitted goods, but without paying duty or completing the necessary paper work (*Doc. 14*). And while he insisted that it was a way of reducing British bullion reserves, Napoleon himself even agreed to permit licensed trade with Britain. Initially this was seen as a way of reducing a French wine surplus, but in 1810 it involved the sale of grain and from that year the sale of such licences clearly began to be seen as an additional way of raising funds.

The years 1807 to 1810 were good for the French economy and, overall, manufacturing expanded. Then came difficulties brought about by a financial crisis in the banking sector across Europe. Banks called in their loans and refused new credit. Manufacturers found themselves with goods they could not sell and began to reduce production and lay off their workers. At the same time, Napoleon's attempt to tighten up the enforcement of his customs regulations worsened the crisis. Recovery, beginning in 1811, was slow and the economy was hit hard again by the military crisis that followed the disastrous Russian campaign.

CENTRALISATION AND SURVEILLANCE

The administrative structure of France had been rationalised during the Revolution. The country had been divided into, initially, 83 departments, roughly equal in size, wealth and population; each department was then subdivided into districts, cantons and finally communes – the latter being roughly the equivalent of a parish. The number of departments increased during the 1790s, most notably with the annexation of the Austrian Netherlands (Belgium). The administrative structures were reorganised, most significantly in 1795 when the districts were abolished and commissioners (*commissaires*) of the Directory were appointed in each department and in the larger communes to work alongside locally elected administrations. By the time of the coup of *Brumaire* there were 98 departments, but they were not functioning well. Financial management was particularly poor, and ferocious internal disputes undermined the system. The Consulate's remedy was centralization.

The law of 17 February 1800 (28 *Pluviôse* Year VIII) abolished the elective element in local government and replaced the old Directorial commissioner with a new central appointee, the prefect. In place of the elected bodies there were to be advisory councils, who were also to be appointed by the First Consul. The old subdistricts were restored as *arrondissements*, between three and six depending on the department, and each under the direction of a centrally appointed subprefect. The smallest administrative unit was the commune under the direction of a mayor. While the prefects and subprefects were career civil administrators climbing the central government hierarchy, the mayors were local men. The mayors of cities and towns with populations in excess of 5,000 were appointed by the First Consul from a list of local candidates. Those of the 40,000 or so smaller communes were appointed by the departmental prefect.

Ideally the mayor was expected to be a man of some wealth and influence in his locality. He had a key role to play in advising the local population of new laws and changes to the law; part of his municipal budget had to be set aside for subscribing to the periodic *Bulletin des Lois*. He was responsible for various minor law and order tasks, for the upkeep of highways, and, in particular, for the local register of births, marriages and deaths, the *État civil*. These tasks made the post burdensome; it was also unpaid. Overall rather more than 40 percent of mayors were peasants (*cultivateurs*); in the poorer departments, with large numbers of peasant holdings, the percentage was even higher. Another 25 percent were small property owners (*propriétaires* or *rentiers*) who did not work in the fields themselves but in terms of wealth and social prestige were far removed from the departmental *notables*. The mayors were much criticised for being lax and illiterate. Some of them probably were barely literate. Their book-keeping was poor, and sometimes deliberately so, particularly when the details of the *État civil* were so central to the conscription process; the mayor, after all, had to continue to live in the community when the conscripts had gone and when angry and sorrowful parents found themselves in difficulty working the land without their sons. The prefects criticised mayors for their failings, and also for being poor correspondents when written responses were needed. Yet it is also possible that prefects and subprefects heaped criticism and blame on the mayors when this could cover any delays and deficiencies on their own part.

Throughout the Consulate and Empire plans were floated both centrally and by local prefects to improve the communal system, and particularly to amalgamate where tiny communes made finding a mayor especially difficult and the overall administration too diffuse. Little change was made to the basic structure; however, in 1808, when the tenure for mayors appointed in 1800 came to an end, there was a significant purge of the mayors. Many of those first appointed had been local men noted for their service in the revolutionary decade; the appointments had been rushed because the prefects were new to their departments. While research on the new appointments has been limited, it appears that a serious attempt was made in 1808 to appoint men with significant landed wealth: *propriétaires-cultivateurs* replaced simple *cultivateurs*, and there was even a small sprinkling of nobles and former *émigrés*. These new mayors may have played an important part in the reduction of communal resistance to conscription and in limiting the opposition towards the forced sale of communal property (*biens communaux*) to help to finance the war during the desperate military situation in March 1813 (Dunne, 2000).

Whatever future research reveals about the mayoral problems of Napoleon's regime, at the level of *arrondissement* and department the administration appeared to function reasonably well. Prefects and subprefects generally administered their districts competently, could be relied upon to do as they were instructed and also to keep the central government informed of developments within their jurisdiction. When Napoleon's Empire reached its peak this centralised system was to be found in the 130 departments of France and the annexed territories of Belgium, the Netherlands, the Rhineland, Italy, and Switzerland. In addition there were identical structures in the satellite kingdoms of Italy and Westphalia.

The law of 17 February 1800 established a special prefect for the city of Paris, the Prefect of Police. Again this was a centralising move; it, and the subsequent defining legislation, put a government appointee at the head of police administration within the capital and placed the forty-eight *commissaires de police*, one for each of the city's sections (later *quartiers*), directly under his orders. Under the old regime the word 'police' had a very wide meaning and was roughly synonymous with the good administration of a territory, and especially that of a town or city. Napoleon's Prefect of Police, like the old regime's *lieutenant générale de police de Paris*, had a wide range of responsibilities from the supervision of markets to the implementation of building regulations, and from the free flow of traffic to the suppression of crime. His headquarters in rue de Jérusalem had more than a hundred administrators, clerks and specialists in the form of architects, engineers and interpreters. The Prefect of Police also had the key task of suppressing threats to the regime and keeping the Minister of Police informed of public opinion in Paris. Each day he received reports from his subordinate officers, from spies and informers, and prepared an account of occurrences for the minister. The account listed the new arrivals in the city, their professions, their origins, where they were staying – details that were made all the easier to collect by the police requirement that all travellers, whether foreigners or French people travelling outside their own commune, carry passports. Further, the daily account listed the people arrested, and their offence; it also detailed any notable events (*événements*) that had occurred, a category that encompassed accidents, assaults, fires, murders, suicides, any rumours circulating, or adverse reports of public opinion (Emsley, 1987). Paris was exceptional in the degree of police surveillance and reporting, but only in the degree. While scarcely comparable with twentieth-century manifestations, Napoleon's Empire had many of the attributes of a police state (Sibalis, 2001; and see *Doc. 3*), though it was a police state tempered by some of the early liberalism of the Revolution.

The arrest and execution of the duc d'Enghien was an exceptional occurrence in Napoleonic France. There were serious conspirators, but there were also people who got drunk and, in their cups, blurted out annoyance with some aspect of the regime or referred to the First Consul, and later the Emperor, disrespectfully – among the most common forms of abusing Napoleon was to corrupt his name to 'Bonneatrappe' (and see *Doc. 2b*). The usual method of dealing with the latter kind of offender was to hold the person for a period of preventive detention, eventually (sometimes after a period as long as two months) releasing him or her without trial. The authorities recognised that a trial could serve to advertise and inflame matters; and with more serious political offenders there was always the concern that a jury might acquit. Preventive detention was used for a variety of offenders from the political conspirator and turbulent priest, to libertines and disorderly children whose families wanted them 'corrected', to habitual thieves and vagabonds. The system might be said to have its origins in the *lettre de cachet* of the old regime, but preventive detention in Napoleonic France possessed a few safeguards inspired by the Revolution's ideas of liberty. The small print of the Consulate's constitution provided for a Senate Commission on Individual Liberty. The commission had a rotating membership of seven senators. It received petitions from prisoners and could require the police or the justice ministry to bring an individual to court; it could even bring a case before the entire senate if it was dissatisfied with the response to its demands. No case was ever taken this far, but the commission did not simply acquiesce in the activities of the police; in its first four months it brought about a release in 44 of the 116 petitions it had received. The number of petitions declined after about 1808, and from 1810 a system of annual review was introduced for all State prisoners. Napoleon considered that he had to have the ability to imprison, if necessary without trial, individuals who presented a threat to the regime. At the same time, he also wanted a rational system that functioned within a legally regulated framework. Neither the Emperor nor his supporters sought to preside over a gulag into which suspects and offenders disappeared and were forgotten (Woloch, 2001a: ch. 7).

At the centre of the Napoleonic police system was the Ministry of General Police. This received regular reports from across the Empire and prepared digests of the contents for Napoleon. Joseph Fouché was the most able of the Ministers of Police. A former lay teacher for the Oratorians, then Jacobin terrorist, he had been Minister of Police under the Directory and had sided with the conspirators of *Brumaire*. His ministry was suppressed and its functions taken over by the Ministry of Justice in September 1802, possibly because he was strongly opposed to the Concordat, and possibly because he was right that the 'Infernal Machine' was the work of Royalists rather than, as Napoleon averred, of Jacobins. However, after less than two years, in July 1804 Napoleon re-established the ministry with Fouché, once again, at its head. In spite of his ability as a police chief, Napoleon never entirely trusted Fouché and never gave him control of all police agencies in the Empire. The most important police instrument outside the minister's control was the Gendarmerie, the military policemen based across the Empire in small barracks each containing from four to six men. The Gendarmerie was responsible first to its Inspector General, Marshal Moncey, and then to the Ministry of War. Fouché and Moncey clashed regularly over procedural matters, and the situation was scarcely any better when Napoleon replaced Fouché with a military man, General Savary, in 1810, following Fouché's secret negotiations with the British. But personal hostilities, jurisdictional clashes, and the division of powers aside, the police organisations of the Empire functioned relatively effectively. They generally kept Napoleon aware of what was going on and of the shifts in public opinion. They could claim much of the credit for bringing internal peace in the aftermath of the Directory. And the Gendarmerie in particular ensured that the conscripts were enlisted and delivered to their muster points (Arnold, 1979; Emsley, 1999).

THE CODE NAPOLÉON

The legal situation in France before the Revolution was extremely complex. Broadly, in the north there was a system of customary or common law, while in the south the old codified Roman Law still functioned. In addition there were some 360 local legal codes. The Revolution swept away the complexities and cleared the way for the creation of a unified legal structure for the country based on Enlightenment rationality. Throughout the 1790s different revolutionary assemblies and governments promised to establish a unified system, but for a variety of reasons all attempts at codification were set aside. It was left to Napoleon to bring these aspirations to fruition with a code that combined many of the achievements of the Revolution with other, more traditional, ideas.

In the summer of 1800, shortly after the victory of Marengo, General Bonaparte selected four legal experts – two schooled in northern practice (François-Denis Tronchet, who had defended Louis XVI before the Convention, and Félix Bigot de Préameneu, who had served as a moderate royalist in the Legislative Assembly and had been imprisoned during the Terror) and two from the south (Jacques de Maleville, a nobleman active as a constitutional monarchist during the Revolution, and Jean Portalis, a moderate veteran of the fraught politics of the Directory) – to draft a Civil Code. At the beginning of 1801 the draft was circulated to the provincial courts for comment, then presented to the legislature and the Council of State for discussion. Radical republicans in the Tribunate were critical that the code stepped back from some of the progressive ideas of the Revolution – criticism that was ignored and contributed to the purge of the Tribunate in 1802. The Commission of Legislation of the Council of State held 102 sessions to discuss the code. The First Consul presided over 57 of these, frequently intervening in the debates; Cambacérès, who had been involved in the codification plans of both the Jacobins and the Directory, presided over the remainder. As the various parts of the code were approved they were issued as laws. On 21 March 1804 these 36 separate laws were unified as the Civil Code of the French People (*Code Civil des Français*); three years later, on 3 September 1807, it was renamed as the *Code Napoléon*.

The Civil Code (*Doc. 6*) maintained the abolition of feudalism and hereditary privilege and the secularisation of the State, all of which had been achieved by the Revolution. Equality before the law and freedom of conscience were corollaries of this. But with these progressive ideas went a traditional, hierarchical and conservative view of the family. The Civil Code declared the father to be the unquestioned head of the family. His children were firmly subordinated to his authority; they could be imprisoned at his request for insubordinate behaviour, and had to seek his permission to marry – daughters until they were 21, sons until they were 25. Legitimate children, however, could not be disinherited, and restrictions on how much property might be freely disposed in a will, meant that three-quarters of a man's property had to be dispersed equally among his legitimate offspring on his death. The latter requirement alleviated some of the problems created by the decision of the Revolution's legislators that an equal division of a man's property should be made – a rule that, especially since it had been made retroactively, had prompted bitter arguments and considerable litigation.

The Revolution had secularised marriage and required a civil ceremony rather than a religious sacrament to ensure legality. But some of the more progressive attitudes towards marriage and towards women that had been given legal sanction during the Revolution, disappeared in the patriarchy of the Civil Code. The ease of divorce granted by the Revolution, for example, was seen as undermining the family. In consequence the Civil Code curtailed the liberal law of 1792. A double standard was introduced for adultery. Under the Civil Code the husband could use it as grounds for divorce whatever the circumstances of his wife's behaviour; but for a wife, adultery was only grounds for divorce if her husband committed the act with his mistress within the family home. The Revolution had never granted political rights to women, and the Civil Code kept them from the public and political worlds. An unmarried woman could have no role in a family council, and could not act as a guardian or witness a legal document. It is significant that a high percentage of Napoleon's interventions during the debates on the Civil Code concerned the position of women, and his comments recorded elsewhere testify to his belief in male superiority. General Gourgaud, for example, reported him as saying on St Helena that women were not equal to men and were best considered as machines for producing children (Herold, 1955: 14). But Napoleon alone cannot be blamed for the misogynist elements of the Civil Code.

Most of the articles in the Civil Code concerned landed property and its possession. It was also supportive of economic liberalism favouring the employer over the employee and continuing the Revolution's policy of limiting the organisation of workers. The Civil Code was followed by four others over the next six years, and these also combined reforms made during the Revolution with more conservative thinking. The Code of Civil Procedure (1806) brought the practice of the courts into harmony with the Civil Code. The Commercial Code (1807) regulated business relations, bankruptcy and debt. In spite of considerable opposition the Code of Criminal Procedure (1808) maintained the practice of jury trials. In part the hostility to juries seems to have been one aspect of Anglophobia. Napoleon himself was unsympathetic to juries but appears to have agreed to their continuance in the expectation that serious trials would go before special courts for which jury selection was controlled by the prefects. The Code of

Criminal Procedure contained a particularly notable backward step in its sanctioning of arrest without trial; and the government's powers in this area were further strengthened by decree in March 1810 but, as noted earlier (see p. 49), the sanction of holding individuals without trial was subject to review. The Penal Code also appeared in 1810, with the death penalty maintained for murder, arson and forgery; in addition, a parricide could suffer the amputation of the right hand before execution. Harsh punishments that echoed those of the old regime, such as branding, or life sentences with hard labour, were also included in the new code. However, the idea of maximum and minimum, rather than fixed penalties, continued the liberal reformist programme of the early stages of the Revolution. Finally, a Rural Code was drafted, but was never implemented. The problems of establishing a rational, uniform structure on the relationships and practices of rural France were too great even for Napoleon's regime to hope to resolve.

CHURCH AND SCHOOL

Napoleon was not noted for any marked, personal commitment to religion. 'I am assuredly very far from being an atheist,' he told Las Cases, 'but I cannot believe all that I am taught in spite of my reason, without being false and a hypocrite' (Las Cases, 1823: ii, 130). But as well as winning and maintaining the support of the *notables*, Napoleon was also keen to secure the backing of the Catholic faithful. He considered religion to be important principally for its role in preserving the social order. He declared:

> Society cannot exist without inequality of fortunes, and inequality of fortunes cannot exist without religion. When a man is dying of hunger alongside another who stuffs himself, it is impossible to make him accede to the difference unless there is an authority which says to him, 'God wishes it thus; there must be some poor and some rich in the world, but hereafter and for all eternity the division will be made differently' (Quoted in Holtman, 1967: 123–4).

Squabbles about the respective authority of the King of France and the Pope in Rome had recurred throughout the old regime. During the eighteenth century the social role of the Church had begun to give place before institutions of the State. In Paris, for example, the *lieutenant général de police* and his agents took over an increasing amount of the pastoral and poor relief roles traditionally undertaken by the clergy. And then the Revolution resolved the Church–State rivalry and curtailed the Church's social role abruptly and decisively. The clergy were required to swear an oath of loyalty to the nation, which drove many into the ranks of counter-revolution. De-Christianisation and other policies introduced by radical Jacobins removed the clergy from poor relief, from keeping the registers of births, marriages and deaths, and from providing much of the education in the country. But religious faith was not stamped out. Indeed, there is evidence that many non-juring clergy survived the persecution of the revolutionary decade and that some regions of France, especially the west, witnessed a strengthening of faith, especially among women who boycotted unpopular constitutional clergy while sheltering non-juring priests, attended secret ceremonies, and put pressure on local authorities to reopen parish churches.

As First Consul, General Bonaparte was eager to remove the Church as a support for the exiled Bourbons. He believed further that reconciliation with the Church would assist in the pacification of the west and the better integration of the staunch catholic peoples of the newly annexed territories of Belgium, Piedmont and the Rhineland. In December 1799 he decreed that churches might open every day of the week, and six months later he authorised the recognition of Sunday, once again, as a day of rest rather than the rational revolutionary regulation of a rest day every tenth day, the *décadi*. That same summer he began the process which, after difficult and lengthy negotiations, resulted in the Concordat with the newly elected Pope, Pius VII.

The Concordat was agreed in the summer of 1801, but not published until Easter Sunday, 8 April 1802. The formal publication date was a significant day in the Christian calendar, but it also suited the First Consul. He had conducted the negotiations in secret because of potential hostility from liberal intellectuals and from the Jacobin elements still to be found in the army and in most of the big ministries, and he hoped that the successful conclusion of the Peace of Amiens with Britain would draw the teeth of any criticism on publication. The Concordat itself gave the First Consul much more than it gave the Pope. The new regime was recognised by the Pope, and the First Consul recognised that Catholicism was the religion of the majority of French citizens. The existing clergy were required to resign and be reappointed; they were to be nominated by the First Consul and consecrated by the Pope. But the French State was to pay their salaries, and this tied them ever closer to the new regime. The Concordat stipulated further that the Church property seized during the Revolution would remain with those individuals who had purchased it (*Doc. 4a*). An additional document, the Organic Articles, was prepared by the First Consul and appended to the Concordat without any consultation with the Pope. The Organic Articles strengthened the State's grip on the Church in France, requiring government approval of any legate sent by the Pope and any document sent by the Pope for publication in the country. Seminaries were to be regulated by the government, and all the teachers in them were to be Frenchmen professing loyalty to Gallican principles (*Doc. 4b*).

The Pope, however, was not just a spiritual leader. Within five years of the publication of the Concordat Napoleon was furious with the Pope for his inability to close the ports of the Papal States to the British and his refusal to enter into a formal alliance. The Pope, in turn, disliked the way that the French were spreading the Concordat down the Italian peninsula. In 1808 French troops occupied Rome; the following year the papal territories were annexed and the Pope was arrested – to which the Pope responded by excommunicating Napoleon. A new Concordat was prepared giving Napoleon even greater say in the administration of the Church, and in January 1813 the Pope was compelled to sign it. The deteriorating military situation meant that this 'Concordat of Fontainebleau' (*Doc. 4c*) was never implemented; moreover, the Pope rapidly repudiated his agreement on the grounds that it was made under duress. The ever worsening of relations between Napoleon and Pius VII did not have significant repercussions within France, but they did elsewhere in the Empire (see below, pp. 68–9).

The Concordat of 1801–02 recognised Catholicism as the religion of most French people. At the same time, however, the First Consul issued another set of Organic Articles that publicly recognised the Protestant communities within France and in 1804 the Civil Code guaranteed freedom of conscience. These moves encouraged Protestants, who were especially prominent in commerce and situated chiefly in the east and south of France, to accept their equal recognition as fellow citizens and to take a more active part in public life.

Jews, the other significant religious minority within France, were especially prominent in Alsace. Napoleon's personal attitudes were tinged with a traditional anti-semitism, yet he also sought assimilation for the Jews within French society. In February 1807 he summoned 45 rabbis and 26 laymen from across the Empire to meet in a Grand Sanhedrin. The body was not as compliant as he had hoped and was wary of his proposals for greater assimilation, particularly his desire to see a much greater number of mixed marriages. Nevertheless, Napoleon's policies, which can be seen as continuing those of the liberal period of the Revolution, did bring about a greater civic assimilation. They set the Jewish faith on something of a par with Christian denominations, though without the State providing funding for rabbis as it agreed to do for Catholic priests and Protestant pastors (*Doc. 5*).

During the Revolution the Church had lost its dominant role in education. The revolutionaries sought to replace the Church with improved and extend schooling reaching out to all future citizens, boys and girls. The aspirations were never matched in practice and the educational system that the Consulate inherited from the revolutionary regimes was in a sorry state. As First Consul, and subsequently as Emperor, Napoleon embarked on a programme of educational reform. In comparison with the aspirations of the revolutionaries it was relatively traditional, yet, in keeping with the ideas of the Enlightenment, it was wholly secular and predominantly scientific in its way of thinking. The reform was limited principally to the education of boys at secondary level. The one notable achievement regarding women's education was the creation, in 1807, of a national system for the training of midwives – a move demonstrative of the regime's overall attitude to women and their role in society.

The law of 11 *Floréal* Year X (1 May 1802) outlined the new educational system for France. Primary schools were to be established in the communes, and inspected regularly by the local subprefect. Private primary schools were permitted, but this was essentially because the law was silent on the subject and because the restoration of private church-run schools was popular. With Napoleon's blessing the Christian Brothers (*les Frères des Écoles Chrétiennes*) played a key teaching role in these schools and similar female congregations were authorised to work in schools for girls over the next few years. But primary education, and the education of girls, were incidental to Napoleon's reorganisation of schooling. The most significant institution created by the law of 11 *Floréal* was a new form of secondary school, the *lycée*.

Napoleon's intention was a centralised educational system that would train young men for civil and military leadership. Scholarships were offered by open competition for places in the 45 *lycées* eventually established across the Empire, but rather more than one-third of these places were reserved for the sons of soldiers and officials. If careers were open to talent, the talented were essentially expected to be found among the sons of *notables*, of those already serving the regime, or of those possessed of small property who were already being wooed by Napoleon. The *lycées* employed strict military discipline; the teaching and administrative staffs were to be centrally appointed; the curriculum was centrally approved, and replaced much of the traditional humanism with a more modern and scientific orientation. The *lycées* were not especially popular, partly because of their discipline, and many fathers appear to have wanted an element of the old religious education for their sons and to have preferred, in consequence, the municipal secondary schools (*collèges*). Financial levies imposed on students in the *collèges* helped the development of the *lycées*, but the *lycée* scholarships were not all taken up.

The Imperial University was announced in May 1806 and formally established by decree in March 1808 with the intention of providing properly trained teachers who were loyal to the regime. It was modelled directly and deliberately on the University of Turin that had earlier developed the intellectual and administrative élite of the Savoyard monarchy, which was greatly admired by Napoleon. The Imperial University itself was not intended to be an institution of teaching and learning in the modern understanding of the word, but rather an instrument for the supervision of teaching throughout the Empire. It was to have a monopoly of teacher training; all appointments and promotions of teachers required its authorisation, as did the creation of new schools. The University was to be directed by a Grand Master who reported annually to Napoleon. Louis de Fontanes, a celebrated literary figure with a chequered revolutionary past, was selected as Grand Master. And while Fontanes had rallied to Napoleon, returning from exile in London at the beginning of the Consulate, he did not implement the secular aspirations for education that Napoleon appears to have favoured. He gave posts in both the *lycées* and the *collèges* to clergy; in 1812 just under a third of the personnel in these institutions were priests or ex-priests. In part this was because of a shortage of qualified teachers, but it appears also to have been because of Fontanes's own thinking and beliefs.

DISSENT AND DISORDER

After the plots of the Consulate, and with the shocking exception of General Malet's near successful coup in 1812, political opposition in France remained relatively subdued during the Empire. Royalist insurrection in the west petered out, and what remained became little distinguishable from brigandage. There were other plots, such as the *conspiration du Midi*, which brought together both republicans and royalists in and around Marseilles and Toulon during the years 1809 and 1813, but failed when it attempted to stage a revolt in the spring of 1813. There were other institutions, sometimes ostensibly charitable bodies, that did not organise plots but rather chipped away at the regime from within. The *Congrégation* was organised by an ex-Jesuit in 1801 to undertake charitable work and to offer particular devotions to the Virgin Mary. But Napoleon's worsening relations with the Pope prompted some of its members into political activity, notably the publishing of the Bull of Excommunication against Napoleon and those who had taken part in the abduction of Pius VII. The *Chevaliers de la Foi* (Knights of the Faith) was established by Ferdinand de Bertier de Sauvigny, a young nobleman briefly arrested for his activities with the *Congrégation*, was outwardly a charitable body, but had a clandestine political agenda. It was organised in 1810 and had a masonic structure; Bertier de Sauvigny had taken to heart the notion that the French Revolution was essentially the fruit of a conspiracy by Freemasons. But the *Chevaliers* were never going to bring down the regime on their own, and nor were the various liberal and religious critics who constituted an irritant, but never a direct threat to Napoleon.

Napoleon expressed frustration that the most celebrated authors living under his regime could rarely be found writing in its favour. The vicomte de Chateaubriand and Madame de Staël are the best remembered of such authors. Chateaubriand came from a noble family in Normandy and had rallied to the First Consul. His *Le Génie du Christianisme* (*The Genius of Christianity*) provided support for the Concordat but, appalled by the execution of the duc d'Enghien, Chateaubriand resigned his government post. In 1807 he published an article in his journal, *Le Mercure de France*, which reflected on the power of the historical critic over the tyrant. D'Enghien was not mentioned, and Tacitus and Nero replaced Chateaubriand and Napoleon, but the meaning was transparent enough. *Le Mercure* was closed and Chateaubriand was banished from Paris. Germaine de Staël was the daughter of Jacques Necker, a Genevan banker and popular finance minister to Louis XVI. She had established a glamorous salon in Paris during the Directory, and continued it during the Consulate. Here she and liberals like her lover, Benjamin Constant, condemned the increasing authoritarianism of the First Consul, lauded representative government and the constitutional structure of Britain, and stressed the superiority of Protestantism over Catholicism. De Staël and her coterie had no popular following and lived by the pen rather than the sword. Nevertheless, in 1803 the First Consul had had enough and she was forbidden to come within a 40 leagues radius of Paris. In 1808 she submitted her book, *De l'Allemagne* (*On Germany*) to the censor. It was condemned as un-French, and she was forced into exile. Yet, if the Jacobins and royalists were largely quiet, and if liberal voices within France were largely silenced, the regime remained concerned about these and other groups within the population. Moreover, several of its key policies served to foster dissent and, occasionally, even violent disorder.

Non-agricultural workers made up only about 6 or 7 percent of the total worker (*ouvrier*) population, but in the big cities they could be roughly half of the inhabitants and they were eyed warily. During the Revolution workers' associations and combinations by employers and employees had been banned. The law of 22 *Germinal* Year XI (12 April 1803) reiterated the bans with particular reference to attempts to bring about changes in wages and hours of work. The Penal Code of 1810 preserved the intention of the law and stiffened the penalties that could be imposed on strike leaders – two to five years in prison as opposed to a mere three months. The law of 22 *Germinal*, and the subsequent decree of 9 *Frimaire* Year XII (1 December 1803), imposed further controls on *ouvriers* by requiring that they carry a *livret*, a passbook. The *livret ouvrier* was issued by the police or the municipality and had to be surrendered to an employer when a person was employed by him. A new employer was forbidden to hire any person whose *livret* had not been signed by the previous employer to certify that all of the person's obligations had been fulfilled. Certain manual labourers, such as porters, water carriers, sweeps, were not required to possess a *livret*, but, while at work, these people had to wear numbered badges supplied by the police and local authorities. These controls were unpopular and seem often to have been circumvented; they did not prevent organisation and industrial action by workers, though they probably impeded it.

As with other societies of the period the bulk of the population of

Napoleonic France was heavily dependent on certain foodstuffs, especially bread. The authorities, through the police, sought to maintain the regular supply of bread at an affordable level. Generally speaking they were successful, and they were assisted in this by overall gains in real wages, assisted by the labour shortages generated by constant warfare. Nevertheless, economic crises and upsets in the grain markets caused by bad harvests provoked disorder, and this was most apparent when the two were combined, as during the years 1811–13. In 1811 and 1812 large numbers of beggars and vagrants, sometimes aggressive, tramped the roads, while food riots erupted in some towns, most seriously in Caen where textile workers and laundresses, supported by conscripts, attacked grain barges, mills and stores. The fears of the authorities were worsened in Caen by the circulation of seditious rumours and fears that the example of English Luddites was about to spread across the Channel (Cobb, 1970: 112–14).

It is always difficult to measure the amount of law-breaking in a society. However, two forms of resistance to the law stand out in Napoleonic France and across the Empire. These were not directly connected to royalist or republican activity. They did not involve strikes by workers, or food riots, but were the result of, first, the disaffection created by the demands of military conscription and by indirect taxes and, second, the opportunities for smuggling created by the Continental Blockade and Napoleon's economic system.

A form of conscription had been created in Revolutionary France in the desperate, early stages of the war against the European powers. But it was the law of 19 *Fructidor* Year VI (5 September 1798 – known as the *loi Jourdan* after General Jourdan who introduced it) that first established conscription on a systematic basis. The law affected young men aged between 20 and 25; a man entered into the first class likely for conscription when aged 20, and continued to be liable for call until the fifth class when he was 25. Classes were called up according to necessity, and not every member of every class would necessarily be required. Thus, in theory, a man could escape altogether if he reached 26 and had not been called. However, between Year VII and 1813 more than 2 million men were recruited under this legislation, and while the system clearly worked and improved as time went on, the annual tax on young men was never popular. Mayors doctored the *État civil*; young men were found elderly wives in order to escape the recruiting sergeant; some cut off a trigger finger or knocked out the front teeth needed to bite, and thereby load, a musket cartridge. Young men ran away or went into hiding; they fought the gendarmes responsible for bringing in the conscripts, often aided by their community (*Doc. 8*). Resistance brought repression, worst of all the *garnisaires* by which troops were quartered on, and at the expenses of, the parents of refractory conscripts in the hope that this would force the reluctant soldiers into the army. The violence and the resistance varied from department to department, and in some of the poorer departments, where the problem was worst, the *garnisaire* was of little use since the peasants could neither pay fines nor pay for the troops quartered on them. The government responded with mobile columns (*colonnes mobiles*) sweeping through villages to root out refractory conscripts and deserters in homes, barns, outhouses, open fields and woods. In France proper the opposition appears to have been worn down by these punitive actions and by the sheer bureaucratic routine of the annual demands. Just when Napoleon's need for conscripts began to increase, from 1811, so the resistance became less and less noticeable. This apparent acceptance of conscription may have stiffened his determination to carry on fighting in the late autumn of 1813 and to issue new calls for men. The conscription demands of November 1813 reversed the trend of the preceding years: there was mass avoidance, mass desertion, and rioting (Woloch, 1986; Forrest, 1989).

The incidence of fraudulent trafficking and smuggling has been investigated piecemeal. However a brief glance through the police bulletins of the period that have been published reveals a considerable degree of both kinds of law-breaking (*Doc. 14*). Many in France were particularly incensed by the restoration of a salt tax in April 1806. Salt was an essential preservative and the old regime tax, the *gabelle*, had created considerable resentment and provoked widespread avoidance and smuggling. Moreover, the new tax under Napoleon was now applied uniformly across the country, even in those regions that, before 1789, had been exempt. It was beyond France, however, in the wider Empire, that hostility to conscription, to the new and more efficient forms of taxation, and to the implementation and enforcement of the Continental Blockade combined with other resentments to generate the most serious, if spasmodic protests.

Many of the reforms carried out during the Consulate and Empire are redolent with the Enlightenment and its rationality. Some built on the ideas and aspirations of the men of 1789, and on attempts by the Directory to restore a sense of order and stability to France. But Napoleon's reforms often took a more conservative line than those dreamed of by the liberal revolutionaries of 1789. And, liberal or not, an underlying, unifying element to many, perhaps most of the reforms – whether the centralised administration, the guarantees of the inviolability of private property, the bringing on of men of talent with little reference to birth – was the desire to foster and maintain loyalty to the regime. The hopes of fostering and maintaining loyalty were dashed, but many of the reforms – the Civil Code, the Bank of France, the metallic currency, the prefectorial system, and others – long outlived the regime by a century and more.

CHAPTER FOUR

REORGANISING EUROPE

Thomas Nipperdey began his acclaimed history of nineteenth-century Germany with the words, 'In the beginning was Napoleon' (Nipperdey, 1996: 1). A similar statement might be made with reference to nineteenth-century Italy. Napoleon dominated continental Europe for over a decade; he understood the new system of mass, conscript armies and how to use them, while his principal German opponents for a long time hung back, reluctant to face up to the new style of war. Across those territories that were directly subject to his will, he introduced similar reforms and established the administrative and government structures that he had overseen in France. He required his satellites, and persuaded his allies, to introduce similar changes. Some of these changes were supported by subject peoples and allies, especially by non-French princes and bureaucrats imbued with Enlightenment ideas for the rational reform of government and administration, as well as by others who saw the reforms working to their advantage. But Napoleon's presence, that of his armies, his constant demands for conscripts and money, and his determination to pursue an economic policy that meant ruin for many areas of his Empire as well as for some of his allies, also fostered unrest, law-breaking and elements of anti-French feeling, especially among the popular classes.

THE SCOPE OF THE EMPIRE

Napoleon ruled France for 15 years and was an Emperor for roughly a decade. His 'Empire' had France as its heart, but its borders were never static for long. There had been 83 departments when France was reorganised by the revolutionaries in 1790. When General Bonaparte became First Consul there were 98. These now included a cluster of *pays réunis*, 14 departments that had been established out of the former Austrian Netherlands (mostly modern Belgium), parts of Switzerland, and various territories bordering the Rhine. Six Piedmontese departments, later reduced to five, were similarly annexed in 1802. More Italian departments were added

57

between 1805 and 1810, followed by the Netherlands and territory in north-west Germany. The Illyrian Provinces were formally acquired from Austria by the Peace of Schönbrunn in 1809; these were never reorganised into imperial departments but, linked with the kingdom of Italy, they made the Emperor master of most of the Adriatic coastline. In 1812, at its territorial peak, Napoleon's Empire consisted of 130 departments with a total population of about 44 million people.

In addition to the formal Empire there were satellite kingdoms. The kingdom of Italy had close associations with Napoleon from its origins. The army of Citizen General Bonaparte was instrumental in establishing the Cispadane, subsequently enlarged into the Cisalpine Republic in Lombardy in 1797. Two years later the republic was destroyed by the Second Coalition. The First Consul restored it, and in January 1802 it was proclaimed the Italian republic by a group of carefully selected Lombard delegates meeting in Lyons under the watchful eyes of a French army. The First Consul was appointed as the republic's president. It seemed incongruous to Napoleon that he should continue to be the president of a republic after he had been crowned Emperor of the French and, in consequence, the Italian republic was transformed into a kingdom. There was some consideration of giving the crown to his brother, Joseph, but in the end Napoleon arranged to be crowned King of Italy himself, in Milan in May 1805. He handed over the administration of the kingdom to his loyal and capable stepson, Eugène de Beauharnais. Early in the following year imperial troops occupied Naples and on this occasion the crown was given to Joseph. Naples was seen as key to limiting British power in the Mediterranean; but the Neapolitan Bourbons, while thrown out of their mainland territories, remained established on the island of Sicily, and with them remained the British. Joseph himself remained 'French' in as much as he also held French titles, including that of Grand Elector of the Empire, and he depended on French troops. Even so he succeeded in establishing a degree of independence for his kingdom, in securing some financial aid from imperial coffers, and he procrastinated over reforms demanded by his brother. Following Napoleon's reshuffle of 1808 Joseph's successors, Marshal Murat and his wife, Napoleon's sister Caroline, had rather less room for manoeuvre, not least because Murat knew that he was suspected of involvement in the machinations of Fouché and Talleyrand. The French presence in the Neapolitan kingdom was reduced and more local men were appointed to the higher levels of government; but the reform programme that Napoleon wanted – the introduction of the Civil Code and conscription – was accelerated. Joseph, in the meantime, was elevated to another, more prestigious former Bourbon throne, that of Spain.

During the decade of the French Revolution Italy had been a battleground for the French and Habsburg armies, and the French had taken some initial, often ephemeral steps at reorganising the old structure of kingdoms, principalities, dukedoms and republics. In the ten years following the coup of *Brumaire* Italy was newly divided and transformed into a series of Napoleonic provinces and fiefs. Running across the north and down the eastern side of the peninsula to the River Tronto, was the kingdom of Italy. This was made up of the old Republic of Venice, the former Habsburg territory of Lombardy and other bits and pieces. In the north-west, Piedmont, the mainland kingdom of the House of Savoy, and the old Republic of Genoa had been incorporated into France. Beyond that, and meeting the kingdom of Italy in the Apennines, were a series of new imperial departments carved out of principalities, dukedoms, the kingdom of Etruria (Tuscany, annexed in 1808) and the Papal States (annexed in 1809). The southern end of the Italian boot was Murat's (King Gioacchino Napoleone's) kingdom of Naples.

When Joseph was crowned King of Spain and the Indies at Burgos on 7 July 1808 two other brothers, Louis and Jerome, were already established respectively in the kingdoms of Holland and Westphalia. The Dutch United Provinces had been reorganised into the Batavian Republic by French arms during the Revolution. Napoleon considered that it was not pulling its weight within his developing continental system and, early in 1806, he contemplated annexation. However, he was then engaged in negotiations with both the British and the Prussians and he recognised that annexing the Dutch provinces could jeopardize his diplomacy. Creating a new kingdom seemed less likely to antagonise the governments in London and Berlin, and Louis was crowned King of Holland in June 1806. Louis's attempts at independence were not treated as leniently as those of Joseph in Naples; he was, after all, a younger brother, he was a semi-invalid and a hypochondriac, but he was also kind, generous and quite lacking in the single-minded toughness of Napoleon. The Netherlands under Louis always seemed to Napoleon to be a weak link in his attempt to keep British goods out of Europe. He criticised his brother and subordinated him to French generals. In the summer of 1810, humiliated by Napoleon's treatment of him and his kingdom, Louis abdicated in favour of his eldest son. Napoleon refused to accept the terms of the abdication and simply incorporated the entire kingdom into the formal Empire.

The kingdom of Westphalia was made up of territory taken from various German princes who had fought Napoleon in 1806–07. The Duchy of Brunswick and the old Electorate of Hesse formed its core, and to this were added those parts of Prussia west of the River Elbe, southern Hanover, which was an hereditary territory of the King of England, and various other small parcels of land. Jerome Bonaparte, the youngest of the brothers, was something of a playboy. But he also proved to be completely loyal to Napoleon and many of his Westphalian troops also remained loyal well into 1814 and many months after the kingdom of Westphalia had itself collapsed.

Though it did not have a Bonaparte as its ruler, the Grand Duchy of Warsaw was similar in many ways to the satellite kingdoms. It was formed out of Polish territories seized from Prussia following the war of 1806–07 and, like the kingdom of Westphalia, its creation was sanctioned by the Tsar during his meeting with Napoleon at Tilsit. The King of Saxony, initially an ally of Prussia but who had signed a separate peace treaty with Napoleon in 1806, was appointed Grand Duke. However, the administration of the duchy was supervised by an executive committee of Polish nobles under the direction of a French resident.

As with Italy, Napoleon's redrawing of frontiers had a significant impact on Germany, though his personal dominance of the structure at the height of his power was not quite as apparent. Again changes had begun during the Revolution as French troops overran the Rhineland. Before the Revolution this area had been a myriad of dukedoms, bishoprics, independent cities, and independent territories of imperial knights of the Holy Roman Empire. There was no tradition of state building, and little promise of it materialising. The French revolutionaries began to bind the left bank of the Rhine together, but the situation remained chaotic until the First Consul took a grip on the new departments of Mont-Tonerre, Rhin-et-Moselle, Roër and Saar and imposed the same administrative system as in France, with a thinly veiled criticism of previous French control. As with the annexed departments of Belgium and Piedmont, the new system functioned reasonably well for the duration of Napoleon's rule. The Rhinelanders on the left bank supported the relatively successful suppression of brigandage, though they continued smuggling, breaking both Napoleon's blockade and economic policies. Their smuggling activities were dealt with relatively leniently by the imperial courts that were staffed by their fellow citizens. Overall, the Rhinelanders found the administrative and legal structures of the French Empire congenial (Rowe, 1999).

Across the Rhine was a row of allies – old duchies enlarged into kingdoms or principalities by the amalgamation of smaller entities from the old Holy Roman Empire. The reorganisation was principally achieved by the *Reichsdeputationshauptschluss*. Following the Peace of Lunéville the Austrians abdicated any responsibility for the reorganisation of the territories of the Holy Roman Empire to a deputation of imperial delegates who met with French representatives between the summer of 1802 and February 1803. The result was a massive reorganisation of the right bank of the Rhine and beyond: 112 independent estates, 66 ecclesiastical territories and 41 free imperial cities disappeared into, and made much larger a cluster of medium sized kingdoms, principalities and duchies. The main beneficiaries were the Grand Duchy of Baden, and the kingdoms of Bavaria and Württemberg. The princes and chief ministers of these states, and of the few others that survived the changes, used the patronage of Napoleon and the disintegration of the Holy Roman Empire as the opportunity for increasing the size of their territories and for extending their authority at the expense of the gentry and the church. They also introduced far reaching reforms in state structure and administration, some of which had been mooted in eighteenth-century Enlightenment thought, but much of which was also similar to that in revolutionary and imperial France. These were the states that, in 1806, Napoleon brought together as the core of the Confederation of the Rhine (*Rheinbund*). This was designed in the hopes of developing some sort of unity and a governmental and administrative structure on French lines in western and southern Germany (*Doc. 7*). Within their individual states most of the rulers carried through reforms along the same, broadly Napoleonic lines. The Confederation itself, however, scarcely progressed beyond a military alliance, yet this provided a formidable addition to Napoleon's forces and especially after it reached its peak in 1810 with a succession of additions, most notably the kingdoms of Saxony (December 1806) and Westphalia (November 1807). The imperial army that invaded Russia in 1812 included 26,000 Saxons, 25,000 Bavarians, 13,600 Württembergers, 7,600 troops from Baden, and a further 17,500 from the smaller states.

As Napoleon established the Confederation of the Rhine, so the Habsburg Emperor formally acknowledged the end of the old Holy Roman Empire. Francis II, already having assumed the title of hereditary Emperor of Austria so as to ensure his parity with the Emperor of the French and the Tsar of Russia, became Francis I of Austria in August 1806. Francis's Empire was to continue for another hundred years. Napoleon's Empire collapsed in a decade. As will be apparent from the resumé above, some parts were only very briefly incorporated, provided with the imperial bureaucracy of prefects, subprefects, tax collectors, customs officers, police *commissaires* and gendarmes, and fully integrated into the system run from Paris. Michael Broers has suggested the nomenclature of 'inner' and 'outer' Empire to differentiate between the imperial territories existing before, and those acquired after 1806. The latter – Spain, the Illyrian provinces, and the north German and central Italian departments – at best were difficult to control and were sometimes centres of insurrection. But Broers also notes further complexities within the Empire and he characterises some areas as 'intermediate zones'. These were territories that, while incorporated before 1807, were never fully reconciled to the Napoleonic regime; the Neapolitan kingdom provides a good example. Finally, he stresses also that some of the most recalcitrant regions of the Empire were situated in what had been France since long before the Revolution – the eastern Pyrenees, Brittany, and the Vendée. 'If Spain was the official imperial ulcer,' he suggests, 'the western march [the Vendée], within "old France" was its unmentionable hernia' (Broers, 2001a: 147; and see also Broers, 1996).

SUPPORT

Napoléon sought to ensure support within the Empire as a whole in much the same way that he did within France. This meant wooing those possessed of property and guaranteeing that property. It also meant bringing on talented men, rewarding those who had shown their loyalty and giving them a stake in the regime, but a stake that offered social prestige and economic security rather than any political power. Like most of his contemporaries on continental Europe, Napoléon favoured traditional landed wealth as an indicator of social standing. But developing and maintaining support from people possessed of landed wealth led to contradictions within the imperial regime, particularly in the territories acquired after 1806 as a spoils system was introduced to reward loyalty and a blind eye was turned towards activities that tested the limits of his legal code.

Dotations were territories that Napoléon seized in his conquered territories (*pays conquis*), usually the domains of a defeated prince or of the Church, and that were then distributed to whomever he chose as a reward for loyal service. The recipient (*donataire*) swore an oath of allegiance to Napoléon and his regime. The revenues of the *dotation* were to be passed on in the recipient's family, through the male line, in perpetuity. The size of a *dotation* varied in accordance with the rank and dignity of the *donataire*. The latter was not expected to reside on his estate, and he was encouraged to transfer the revenue from his rents to France. This was not another form of feudalism. The recipient did not acquire any of the rights, notably the right to administer justice, that had gone with feudal domains; and, of course, feudalism had been abolished at the outset of the French Revolution. Even so, *dotations* were confined to the outer Empire that had not had a decade or so to experience and absorb the reforms of 1789. The scale of the *dotations* was enormous and the drain on the revenues of the satellite states seriously hampered their internal development. Westphalia was among the territories hardest hit and, in 1810, 4,000 *donataires* were drawing over 10.5 million francs from the kingdom. Both Westphalia and the Grand Duchy of Warsaw lost around 20 percent of their revenues in this way.

Some of the biggest recipients of *dotations* and other imperial honours, such as Joseph, Jerome and Murat, were critical of feudal privilege and took a tough line against it in their kingdoms. However, even where the Code Napoléon was promulgated there continued to be territories in which the process of abolishing aspects of feudalism and seigneurial privilege was at best gradual, and at worst moribund. Sometimes there was a lack of officials keen to enforce the legislation; sometimes compromise seemed the best way of ensuring the loyalty of the élite of landowners, especially in those areas of central and eastern Europe where feudalism seemed more deeply rooted than it had been in France in 1789. In the Grand Duchy of Warsaw, regardless of the introduction of the Napoleonic Code, the position of the peasant remained largely unchanged; but then the support of the proud Polish nobility was of more importance and value to Napoleon than that of the peasantry. In parts of the Confederation of the Rhine many landowners ignored or circumvented the code so as to hang on to their traditional dues and their rights of labour. Yet on the left bank of the Rhine, in the departments annexed to France during the revolutionary decade, the Code became firmly entrenched. Indeed, it was so well entrenched that, after 1815, the Rhenish élite successfully preserved the Napoleonic Code and resisted the attempts of their new Prussian masters to introduce the Prussian *Allgemeines Landrecht*.

When he took over a territory Napoleon was always keen to have information collected on who were the leading families and the most wealthy individuals. There may have been a French cultural imperialism among his bureaucrats, and the civil service in France remained over-whelmingly French, but Napoleon was interested, first and foremost, in loyalty to himself and his regime. This meant that the policy of *ralliement* was encouraged within the Empire. Local men of wealth and social standing were encouraged to take important posts within those imperial territories that had not been part of France before the Revolution. The reforming Lombard nobleman Francesco Melzi played a key role in both the Republic and the kingdom of Italy; and there were similar individuals in Naples (Francesco Ricciardi and Giuseppe Zurlo), in the Netherlands (Rutger Jan Schimmelpenninck), in Westphalia (Ludwig von Bülow), and elsewhere. A man's past was not as important as his wealth, social standing and his loyalty to the system. Among the new administrators in the Rhineland, for example, were men whose families had held land and served in the old Holy Roman Empire, men whose origins and wealth were rooted in commerce, and men who had sided with the radical element of the French Revolution in the early 1790s. As in France itself, there could be problems in getting some of the old nobility to come forward. Melzi, for example, complained of precisely this situation in Italy, and the *ralliement* of the Rhenish nobility was, as in France, more noticeable as the Empire progressed and appeared to be becoming a permanent entity. But situations varied from place to place. In Spain one of the major weaknesses of the Bonapartist kingdom was, arguably, Joseph's failure to bring forward, in any numbers, collaborators of significant wealth and social standing.

Loyalty to the Emperor brought honours. Imperial titles were given to 285 of the leading families of the annexed territories and satellites; 170 of these went to Italians and 70 to Poles, both nationalities with élites that contained men particularly enthusiastic towards the regime. Napoleon appointed a few such similar men to the *Conseil d'État* and the sons of such men were made *auditeurs* and set on the first rung to top posts in the imperial bureaucracy. Young men from good families were also encouraged to make a career and a name in the imperial army. In Italy, military academies were established in Bologna, Lodi, Modena and Pavia. Yet there could be an ambivalence about accepting the honours. Respected families in the new territories of the Empire did not always want their sons packed off to *lycées*, to military academies, or even appointed to the prestigious post of *auditeur*. They often preferred, like some of the old nobility in France, to keep the family's head down and not to be involved with the Napoleonic regime, even as the *ralliement* gathered pace after about 1808. This might create friction within families where the young men were caught up in the Napoleonic military romance or were inspired by what they saw as the progressive benefits of imperial rule. But even some of the men from outside France proper who served the regime loyally could be ambivalent. Cesare Balbo, for example, came from an established family in Piedmont and was singled out for an appointment as an *auditeur*. He greatly admired the French administrative system and was later to develop it for the restored Savoyard monarchy, but he also intensely disliked much that he was required to do for Napoleon and was strongly opposed to French cultural hegemony on the Italian peninsula. The Rhinelander Anton Rebmann had supported the liberalism of the French Revolution, objected to Napoleon's imperial title, but still accepted the *Légion d'honneur*. Rebmann served the Empire as a judge loyally clamping down on bandits but contriving, at the same time, to save the lives of Germans who fought in Major von Schill's attempted nationalist uprising in 1809. On Napoleon's fall he argued strongly for the preservation of French institutions in the Rhineland.

OPPOSITION

While support for the imperial regime was not always wholehearted, the resentment and dislike of it often appears to have simmered rather than manifesting itself openly or violently. Moreover, while opposition to Napoleon has often been described in nationalist terms, much of it came from groups that had little understanding of a political nation. A series of military uprisings in Germany in 1809, notably those of Major von Schill and the Duke of Brunswick, received no popular support. The risings in Italy, Spain and Tyrol, which have often been labelled as popular and nationalist, had complex origins and rarely much of a political agenda that can be comfortably labelled as nationalist in the modern sense.

Nationalism is a concept that is hotly debated by historians and political scientists. Some have seen the beginnings of its modern manifestation in the period of the French Revolution and Napoleon, and the Germans have been particularly singled out for developing a nationalist response to Napoleon. There were men later claimed as national martyrs: the bookseller Palm,

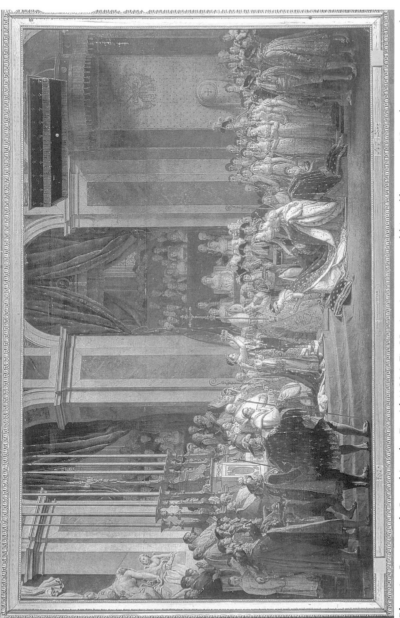

Plate 1 Le sacre de Josephine, by David (1806–7). Having just crowned himself emperor, Napoleon now proceeds to crown Josephine. In addition to painting the Pope's hand raised in blessing and Napoleon's mother, who was absent, David falsified the scene in several other ways. Perhaps most notably, he portrayed Napoleon's sisters as serene and tranquil, when they had visibly sulked at having to carry Josephine's train.

Source: © Photo RMN, Hervé Lewandowski

Plate 2 Napoleon visiting the plague victims at Jaffa, by Gros (1804). General Bonaparte
exudes calm as well as tenderness for the victims. He stretches out his hand as if to heal the
underam buboes of one, a gesture at once Christ-like but also echoing the belief that
medieval monarchs could cure scrofula by touch.
Source: Chantilly, musée Condé © Photo RMN, Harry Bréjat

Plate 3 Napoleon at the battle of Eylau, by Gros (1808). Again, a serene Napoleon holds out his arm as if to bless the dead and dying. A dying soldier in the foreground hails him, while an enemy soldier kisses his boot.

Source: Louvre © Photo RMN, Daniel Arnaudet

Plate 4 The Emperor Napoleon in His Study at the Tuileries by Jacques-Louis David (1812). One of Napoleon's favourite portraits. It suggests that he has been working into the early hours – a candle gutters, the clock says 4.13. His sword is set aside. A scroll headed 'CODE' is on his desk while others tumble on to his chair. Source: Samuel H. Kress Collection, Image © 2003 Board of Trustees, National Gallery of Art, Washington

executed for selling anti-French literature in Nuremberg in 1806; Major von Schill, killed leading his men during his attempt to stage a national uprising; and Friedrich Staps, the student shot for attempting to assassinate Napoleon at Schönbrunn in 1809. There were nationalist intellectuals and teachers like Ernst Moritz Arndt and Johann Gottlieb Fichte. The former was forced into exile for his pamphlets, poems and songs urging the Germans to take up arms against the French. The latter delivered a series of addresses to the German people in the winter of 1807–08 in which he urged them to rouse themselves, reject the self-seeking behaviour which, he claimed, had led to disaster, and forge a new moral bond of national community. There were also the reforming politicians and soldiers who set out to reorganise Prussia in the aftermath of the disaster of 1806: men like Baron Stein, who engineered the political reforms, Hardenberg, who continued them, and Scharnhorst, who rebuilt the army. And there were the Prussian generals, of whom Yorck was the first, who began the trend of turning against Napoleon in defiance of orders after the retreat from Moscow. Yet these men often had very different ideas about patriotism and, at the time, they had a varying impact on their contemporaries. Fichte may have been working towards a romantic, intellectual concept of nationalism, but the French were not much concerned by his philosophical lectures that, after all, drew small audiences. Arndt, and Friedrich Jahn who advocated gymnastics as a means of boosting morale and patriotism and fought the French in the Prussian army and then, in 1813, in the celebrated Lützow Korps, were both too radical in their ideas for the Prussia that emerged in 1815. Stein, for all the reforms that he introduced, was a man who looked back to the old system of the hier-archical Holy Roman Empire in which he had begun his career. Yorck was a conservative feudal landowner. When in 1813, during what became known as the German War of Liberation (*die Befreiungskrieg*), the King of Prussia called upon Germans to fight Napoleon, he addressed them as 'Brandenburgers, Prussians, Silesians, Pomeranians, Lithuanians', not as 'Germans'. He appealed to the people, the *Volk*, not to a nation of citizens who enjoyed, or were expected to enjoy, any kind of political stake in their country.

Austria employed similar propaganda, particularly in the war of 1809. But there was no notion of letting the populace share in, or become involved in the Empire as participatory citizens. The Austrian élite was sensible to the potential danger of encouraging national sentiment given the ethnic mix of its own Empire, but it recognised, nevertheless, the value of using as propa-ganda the example of the popular Spanish uprising of 1808. Yet, even if these were not clear manifestations of a political nationalism, the wars of Napoleon witnessed monarchs and princes, and others in the German lands, making appeals to the people in a way that had not happened before 1789. Similar appeals were made elsewhere to take up arms against the French, but in Italy it tended to be the Bonapartist élite that made appeals to Italians. This was largely successful when directed towards the élite in the kingdom of Italy for most of that satellite's existence. It was spectacularly unsuccessful with Murat's appeal to the Italians to unite behind his Neapolitan army to save his throne during the Hundred Days.

Opposition to Napoleon more commonly sprang from rather more prosaic causes than the nationalism that was so inspiring to many nineteenth- and early twentieth-century historians of the period. The presence of imperial troops was invariably a burden. Napoleon's armies lived off the land and even when payment for requisitions was forthcoming, and even if innkeepers could profit from large numbers of troops with hearty thirsts, large numbers of troops, with their camp followers, were not something generally to be welcomed. Even within the Empire and within their region of recruitment soldiers could be unruly. They squabbled among themselves, rival regiments fought each other, and sometimes they fought or abused townsfolk and country people. The armies brought stragglers, deserters and draft dodgers in their wake. Some of these found succour in, and were hidden by their native communities; some slipped into banditry and brigandage where imperial administrators were rarely the easiest, and therefore rarely the first targets. Some conscripts from the Rhineland departments, and notably in those territories that had previously belonged to the Hohenzollerns, fled across the Rhine, and subsequently turned up fighting in the Prussian army. As Napoleon's German allies began to fall away in 1813, so mistrust led to conscription demands in the Rhenish departments being cut back.

Conscription, improved taxation methods, the blockade and an economic system that favoured some areas, especially French regions, at the expense of others, generated resentment that occasionally erupted into violence. Usually popular protest was confined to a village or a town as the community turned on local officials, a group of gendarmes or customs men. In the summer of 1809, however, brigands linked with the local peasantry to provide a nasty shock for parts of the kingdom of Italy. Unrest began in the Veneto and Upper Lombardy with an Austrian invasion. It became serious in May when peasants in the department of Reno (centred on Bologna), infuriated by a range of new taxes on basic necessities, joined with brigands to destroy tax records, conscription rolls and other legal documents (*Doc. 14b*). The trouble was soon suppressed by the army, but Prince Eugène was careful to exercise clemency to those captured so as not to inflame the situation further (Grab, 1995a). And if the uprising was suppressed the brigandage continued; and so too did the resentment. When the Empire collapsed in 1814 the reforming finance minister of the kingdom of Italy, Giuseppe Prina, was singled out by the crowd in Milan for lynching.

Further down the Italian peninsula there was a constant threat from brigandage. Calabrian peasants, inspired by Cardinal Fabrizio Ruffo, had risen against the short-lived, French-imposed Parthenopian Republic in 1799. The peasantry resented the Bourbon monarchy's failure to meet Ruffo's promises of a reduction in feudal dues and the hated salt tax, but still showed no love for the French when they returned in 1806. Initially there was the problem of French requisitioning. Then King Joseph, followed by King Gioacchino, abolished feudalism and sold off Church lands. This bene-fited existing landowners, but deprived the peasantry of access to grazing, to water courses, and also to the charity and welfare assistance that had been provided by the Church. The brigandage was not nationalist, and was not to restore the Bourbons. It was nourished by the region's tradition of vendetta, and by the occasional British incursion from Sicily. Some of the guerrilla fighters, such as Michele Pezza better known as Fra Diavolo, were to become folk heroes, but many were just as much of a threat to the peasantry as to the French. Ferocious repression by the French resulted in the region being relatively pacified by the beginning of 1811, but the five years of fighting had cost the Empire some 20,000 troops, and there were even more civilian and guerrilla deaths (Finley, 1994). A similar kind of brigand conflict erupted in central Italy around Rome when the Papal States were annexed and the Pope was removed and imprisoned.

The war in Spain, Napoleon's 'Spanish ulcer', has often been described as a popular, people's war against the invaders. Indeed, it was characterised as such from the very beginning by the British who found the conflict in the Iberian peninsula as the best place to wear away at Napoleon with their own, relatively limited military forces. There was a popular uprising in Madrid in May 1808; and other popular uprisings followed in the ensuing weeks. Spanish armies of varying abilities remained in the field for the dur-ation of the conflict. Spanish troops deployed as irregulars and guerrilla bands without military affiliation hit French supply lines, killed dispatch riders and stragglers, and ambushed relatively small, isolated military units. But the mayhem of the Spanish war was hardly a nationalist rising in the accepted sense of the term, and the scale of the popular uprisings of the summer of 1808 was not maintained for the duration of the Peninsular War. Young men from the Spanish countryside were as reluctant to join the Spanish armies as other peasants were to join the imperial armies. Some of the guerrilla bands did become well organised and were even eventually amalgamated with the Anglo–Portuguese–Spanish armies. But self-interest appears to have motivated the leaders of these bands as much as their hatred of the French or any love for their country or their native region; and some of the guerrillas were no different from conventional bandits and as much a threat to the Spanish peasantry as to Napoleonic soldiers. The Napoleonic invasion of Spain unleashed a variety of economic, political, religious and social forces that turned Spaniard against Spaniard, peasant against landowner, liberal against conservative, as much as Spaniard against Frenchman – or German, Italian, or Pole given the various origins of the men serving the Empire in the peninsula (Esdaile, 2004).

The other great popular rising of the Napoleonic period was that in the Tyrol in the summer of 1809. Initially this was not a rising against Napoleon and his Empire, but against his Bavarian ally. During the eighteenth century Tyrol had been a province of the Habsburg Empire enjoying a considerable degree of autonomy. During the 1780s the reforming Emperor, Joseph II, had set about eroding the province's privileges and seeking to erode and suppress some of the extravagant manifestations of its Catholicism; he had backtracked at the end of his reign before a wave of Tyrolean protest. Fighting French revolutionary troops in the 1790s contributed to a transformation of a dislike of Enlightenment reform into counter revolution. During this struggle the Tyrolean people appear to have developed a clear consciousness of their fatherland, and a German cultural identity that was drawn in contrast to stereotypes of Frenchmen and Italians (Cole, 2000). Napoleon ceded the province to Bavaria in 1806, and the reforming government of King Maximilian I Joseph and his chief minister Montgelas took up where the reforming Habsburg had left off. The Tyrolean uprising of 1809 was negotiated with the government in Vienna and was planned to coincide with the new onslaught against Napoleon. But in the eyes of the Tyrolese the uprising was in support of the old privileges, the traditional ways of the Catholic Church, and manifested a continuing hostility towards Protestants and Jews. The relations with Vienna rapidly soured when, following the military successes of Andreas Hofer and his Tyrolean fighters, it became clear that the Austrians would not be content to let the province enjoy the old autonomy. After the Austrians were defeated by Napoleon and had signed the Peace of Schönbrunn, Hofer and his province were isolated and alone. The province was rapidly pacified, though principally by French, rather than Bavarian, troops commanded by Eugène. Hofer was captured and shot (Eyck, 1986).

In the eyes of many ardent Catholics Napoleon's army and regime were not greatly different from those of the radical, anti-Christian Jacobins. This was especially the case when Church lands were seized and sold off by Bonapartist governments and where clerical institutions were closed. Such behaviour, as has been noted above with reference to Calabria, could have both economic and social consequences. It could boost the opportunities for a certain kind of landowner who sought to expand his property and who might then be supportive of the regime. At the same time it could reduce the opportunities for the poorer peasant, particularly when in need of charitable or medical help. In Italy, and especially south of the Bonapartist kingdom, Catholic hostility to Napoleon became extremely marked with many clergy, taking their cue from the Pope, resenting the spread of the Concordat down the peninsula and the French determination to impose their concept of religious toleration. These clergy began putting greater stress on the baroque elements within their faith and playing to the superstitions of the popular classes. In so doing they confirmed French attitudes about the fanaticism, ignorance and decadence in the country. Incidents in Tuscany during Easter 1808, the first Easter that the French were rulers of the region, provide a good, if extreme example of the potential for trouble. The property of some closed clerical orders had recently been sold off as *biens nationaux*. A group of Jews was prominent among the purchasers. The new Prefect of Ombronne was warned that agitators were seeking to rouse the populace against these Jews by emphasising both who the purchasers were, and the loss of charity for the poor and assistance for the sick that would result from the sales. The warnings hearkened back to a pogrom in Siena in 1799. At the same time the Archbishop of Pisa sought to resist the French requirement that the Easter services should omit the traditional condemnation of the Jews for the death of Jesus. The Pope aggravated the situation by publishing a popular prayer book that emphasised the traditional message. In the event there was no serious trouble, but Easter Mass in the churches of Pisa was conducted with French troops deployed alongside the congregations (Broers, 2002: 33–4).

The French may have stood firm and imposed toleration in Italy, but this was not the case everywhere. Jews in Italy may have been protected as fellow citizens in the teeth of popular prejudice and clerical traditionalism, and they responded to this with loyalty to Napoleon; but in the Grand Duchy of Warsaw, as was the case with the Polish peasantry, the 800,000 Jews in the territory were sacrificed to political expediency. The loyalty of the Polish élite in this outer region of the Empire was perceived as the greater need. And if the Pope and many Catholics in Italy, the Tyrol and Spain were hostile because of their understanding of the Napoleonic regime's attitude towards their faith, not all Catholics were similarly hostile. There were men among the Catholic élite who sided with the Empire, often subscribing to the progressive change advocated by the Enlightenment. Karl von Dalberg is the most prominent example. A former leader of the Catholic Enlightenment he had, as Archbishop Elector of Mainz, tried to breathe life into the administrative machinery of the Holy Roman Empire before throwing in his lot with Napoleon and becoming Prince Primate of the Confederation of the Rhine.

Opposition within Napoleon's Empire came from a variety of sources. Much of it sprang directly from his policies – economic, military, religious. Patriotic feelings for a region and hostility to imperial troops as foreigners and outsiders had a role in some of this opposition. Subsequently both the patriotism and the hostility have been labelled, rather ambitiously, as nationalist. But these forms of internal opposition in themselves did not bring about the demise of Napoleon's Empire. His Empire was won on the battlefield and created by the diplomatic aftermath of war; and it was the opposition of external enemies, international war, defeat and diplomacy that brought about his downfall.

The major European wars of the eighteenth century had involved six principal powers: Austria, Britain, France, Prussia, Russia and Spain. Britain had always fought France, and Spain was usually in alliance with France. Austria had usually fought against Prussia. Russia's diplomacy led her to look east as well as west and to seek alliances wherever her interest seemed best served. But eighteenth-century wars were qualitatively and quantitatively small fry in comparison with those unleashed by the French Revolution. The small, professional armies of eighteenth-century princes often had manoeuvred and counter-manoeuvred seeking to outposition an opponent rather than, at the earliest opportunity, deliberately seeking a battle which the weapons and tactics of the time made so costly. Territories might change hands and states might cease to exist; the three partitions of Poland (1772, 1793 and 1795) that led to her disappearance as an entity, provide the most extreme example. But the principal powers remained seemingly inviolable. The French Revolution overturned this situation with its young, ruthless generals and its mass, conscript armies that enthusiastically sought battle and thought nothing of the complete reorganisation of conquered territory and even of the defeated dynasty. In the new climate even the principal powers no longer felt that their existence was safe; and Napoleon's treatment of defeated dynasties contributed to this anxiety.

At different moments Napoleon signed treaties with each of the five other principal powers of Europe, but none was to be a permanent ally. Britain, following the pattern of earlier conflicts, was to be his most consistent enemy. Britain's war policy against Revolutionary France had been confused, and it was not always much clearer during the conflict with Napoleon. She was concerned about the whole Atlantic and North Sea coastlines of Europe coming under French control. She was equally keen to establish and then to maintain maritime and colonial supremacy. This supremacy, together with the products of her developing industries and her highly efficient fiscal system, enabled Britain to act as the major paymaster of the five major coalitions organised against, first, Revolutionary France and then Napoleonic France. Napoleon's recognition of the need to prevent British gold from being used to fund continental armies against him led to his blockade. But the blockade, in turn, generated friction with other powers in Europe and contributed significantly to his entanglement in Spain, and to his decision to embark on the disastrous Russian campaign of 1812.

In 1815, seeking to hold off the military threat from the other monarchs of Europe, Napoleon addressed them in a respectful sense as 'brother' (*Doc. 17*). But over the previous decade he had shown a tendency to treat them as he treated his own siblings rather than as men of equal weight and standing, ruling as members of long-established dynasties. They could work with him as allies, enforce his economic blockade against Britain as he wished, or face the consequences. And the consequences could be harsh. The treaties that he enforced at the end of his wars rarely showed much generosity towards the defeated. This left those who had been defeated with a cause for resentment. Defeat in 1806 cost Prussia a massive indemnity (120 million francs). In addition, she had to pay for the upkeep of French troops garrisoned on the Oder; she lost all of her territories west of the Elbe, and all of the territories that she had acquired in the partitions of Poland a dozen and more years earlier. Defeat cost the Bourbons in Italy half of their kingdom. Napoleon's aggressive diplomacy cost the Spanish Bourbons their entire kingdom. All of this left those who had simply watched the latest conflict or most recent round of diplomatic negotiations uncertain about his future intentions. Francis I, for example, was particularly alarmed by Napoleon's treatment of the Spanish monarchy and feared for his own throne.

The great French historian Georges Lefebvre argued that it was probably impossible to envisage Napoleon as having a positive, precisely defined goal that, once achieved, would have left him satisfied. But he argued further that Europe's kings and princes maintained their hostility to him because they saw him as a parvenu and they had an intense hatred for Revolutionary France in general (Lefebvre, 1969). There is some truth in such conclusions. The Bonapartes did not have the pedigree of the Habsburgs, the Hohenzollerns, the Bourbons, the Romanovs, or the house of Hanover that ruled Britain. Yet being a parvenu did not disqualify a man from acceptance at the high table of monarchs as the career of Bernadotte, Napoleon's former comrade in arms and former marshal, demonstrates. In 1810 Bernadotte became Crown Prince of Sweden, he commanded a Swedish army against Napoleon at Leipzig, and succeeded to the Swedish throne as King Charles XIV in 1818. The diplomatic records show that all of the principal powers were generally prepared to mediate rather than fight, and were motivated by independent state interests throughout the period. Ganging up on Napoleon to restore the Bourbons to France, or simply to get rid of Napoleon, was never their prime aim. Some sought to mediate even towards the end. This was the case with Austria early in 1813, for example. Even then it was not clear to the Austrians that Napoleon's overthrow was on the cards. Nor was it obvious that his defeat and overthrow would be the best policy for them to follow. And they were concerned that an Austrian defeat in another war could be even more costly than it had been in 1809. That said, however, it is at least arguable that compromise was seen less and less as an option when dealing with Napoleon, and especially after his victories in 1805 and 1806 and his subsequent demands and diplomacy.

The Napoleonic Wars and the furious diplomacy of the period have been described as crucial elements contributing to the creation of a new system of international relations within Europe. Paul W. Schroeder has challenged the notion that the Napoleonic Empire could have been maintained for long under someone else's direction, or that it could have developed into an integrated continental European economy. This Empire, he emphasises, depended on colonialism, and 'there was no way to achieve a stabilization of the Napoleonic Empire within the European international system; because the only relationship allowed by Napoleonic France was colonial dependency' (Schroeder, 1994: 394). It took the leading statesmen of Europe some time to recognise this, and for the best part of the first decade of the nineteenth century most of them sought, at least at some point, to make the Napoleonic system work within the existing framework of international relations. By 1813 they had unanimously agreed that this was impossible and at the Congress of Vienna they set about constructing the new international system that was to give Europe its most peaceful and progressive period of international relations. Nineteenth-century Europe was not untroubled by war, but there was to be no international conflict engulfing all of the powers of continental Europe for a century after Napoleon's fall.

CHAPTER FIVE

RESULTS AND MEANINGS

LEGACY

The Congress of Vienna, which redrew the map of Europe in the aftermath of Napoleon's final defeat, did not undo all of the changes wrought by the French Revolution, Napoleon and 25 years of war. The rulers of Austria, Prussia and Russia united in the Holy Alliance to oppose any recurrence of revolutionary ideals and aspirations, and from time to time the great powers deployed their military might to suppress revolution and nationalist uprisings. They continued to eye each other warily, but they also sought to maintain a balance between themselves. Napoleon had treated his defeated opponents harshly. What stands out in the agreement reached at Vienna, and in the way that it was carried through over the next few years, was how differently the victorious allies treated France. Of course some of this was due to the fact that the Bourbon monarchy was restored, some was due to the shrewd diplomacy of Talleyrand, formerly foreign minister to Napoleon and now working for the restored monarchy. But much was also due to a recognition by the allies that, even although it was reduced to almost the frontiers of 1789, France remained, potentially, a great power with considerable economic and manpower resources.

There was no attempt by the powers at Vienna to re-establish the hundreds of tiny states (*die Kleinstaaterei*) that had existed in Germany in 1789 under the umbrella of the Holy Roman Empire. Hence, much of the reorganisation agreed by the *Reichsdeputationshauptschluss* remained in place. Metternich, acting for the Austrian government, was prepared to accept the changes provided that the kings, princes and dukes in the region were prepared to accept Austrian supremacy in a new German Confederation. The kings, princes and dukes, who had seized the chances offered them in the previous decade under Napoleon, had no quarrel with this. They had, after all, scrambled to escape the sinking ship of Napoleon's Empire in 1813 in the hope of preserving their new states. The new arrangements did not mean that they had to give up territory, their new, more efficient French-style administrative structures, or the new authority that French-style reforms had given them over Church and gentry.

Germany was not the only region of Europe where the administrative structures of the Napoleonic Empire were continued under the Restoration. Stuart Woolf has argued that the French–Napoleonic model of a uniform government administration strictly controlled from the centre was one of its most significant and long-lasting legacies (Woolf, 1992). In some areas, in much of Italy for example, the shift from Napoleonic rule to that of a restored or new prince saw little change in the structure of the bureaucratic authority imposed by the French. Tsar Alexander took over the Grand Duchy of Warsaw and kept much of the political, legal and military structure intact, ruling it as a monarchy distinct from Russia. In Spain King Ferdinand, who was violently opposed to any liberal reform, still saw advantages in preserving Joseph's fiscal changes. Victor Emanuel I in Piedmont set out to abolish all vestiges of the French annexation and to restore the old regime, yet he maintained the structure of the French gendarmerie for his *Carabinieri* and also reiterated Napoleonic censorship provisions. The problem for all of the restored princes and their governments was that their predecessors during the Enlightenment had been seeking more efficient ways of organising and administering their territories and, much as they personally may have disliked Napoleon and all that he stood for, he had established 'an apparatus of state … characterized by an unparalleled level of efficiency' (Laven and Riall, 2000: 1). Furthermore, the French regime had introduced new rights, opportunities and equalities while its seizure and sale of property had benefited many property owners. Any attempt to overturn these settlements completely would have resulted in considerable unrest among many articulate and influential individuals. A return to 1789 was simply impossible; what to abolish, what to preserve, and when and how to compromise were the problems for rulers during the restoration.

Yet for all the compromises and the maintenance of French changes and administrative systems, the Restoration period, not least with the signing of the Holy Alliance, gave the impression of being rigidly conservative and reactionary. This atmosphere led to many viewing Napoleon as a liberal. He had, after all, confronted the restored, conservative monarchs. In some territories his administrators and soldiers had established and enforced liberal reforms. He had developed his liberal image in France during the Hundred Days with measures such as the *Acte additionelle*. The liberal Emperor was an image that Napoleon played upon in the memoirs dictated on St Helena. In the decades following his fall some opponents of the restored regimes turned to this image of a liberal Napoleon, the romantic hero and child of the Revolution, as an inspiration for their own liberal aspirations and, particularly in Italy, also for nationalist ones.

ASSESSMENT

An assessment of Napoleon's career has to take account of his role in the internal affairs of France as well as his impact across Europe. With regard to the former there is the central, ever-popular question as to whether he saved the Revolution or perverted it. There is no doubt that he created and presided over an authoritarian regime. Yet it is also apparent, as Isser Woloch has convincingly demonstrated, that some of his authoritarian inclinations were circumscribed by the achievements of the Revolution and by some of his early collaborators, the liberal republicans of *Brumaire* who often succeeded in acting as a brake (Woloch, 2001a). The liberal aspirations of revolutionaries in 1789 were not achieved under Napoleon, but then they had not been achieved in the decade of the Revolution and they were not much favoured by the regime that followed each of his abdications. The Napoleonic regime restored stability. It brought a degree of reconciliation among the warring factions and even a degree of fusion. The regime might have emasculated the representative element in the State. Its legal code with powerful patriarchal domination in matters of family and inheritance may not be to modern taste, but the Civil Code was to last, and it guaranteed the property settlements of the Revolution and some of the equalities sought by it. The regime also established a governing system and an administration that functioned efficiently and successfully. The restored Bourbons took it over and tinkered with it, as did successive regimes, yet the administrative system and structures that were to govern France for the nineteenth and twentieth centuries were essentially those that emerged during the Consulate.

It is possible to debate the extent to which Napoleon's regime alone was responsible for the positive developments of effective government and reconciliation. The desire for ending venality in government posts, for creating a system in which talent counted for rather more than birth and privilege, and for establishing a rational, centralised structure of administration and law were all present and significant in debates towards the end of the old regime. It thus becomes possible to see the years of the Napoleonic adventure as a stage in the evolution of France from a decayed renaissance monarchy into a modern, bureaucratic Nation State. Yet, even from this perspective, the Napoleonic regime has significance. The Revolution had brought a dramatic collapse of the old order. It had also launched a succession of projects based on Enlightenment thinking for legal, political and administrative reform. Napoleon's rule saw some, but by no means all, of these projects brought to some kind of fruition. The acquiescence of the restored Bourbons, and of the people, was required after 1815 to ensure, first, that these projects continued and, second, that France was not immediately plunged, once more into turmoil. Charles X's failed attempt to act out his perception of an old regime absolutist and impose his will in 1830 revealed the extent of the change that had occurred in the French polity. Moreover, while the revolutionary and the Napoleonic regimes left a legacy of rival political groups who, in a political crisis, would step forward with their respective, ideal forms of constitution, the overall, centralised administrative and legal structures, and a legislature selected on a rational basis, remained in place.

Beyond the frontiers of France Napoleon succeeded, momentarily, in creating French military hegemony across Europe. He deployed France's enormous manpower – at that time the largest population in Europe – in the mass armies created by the Revolution. He used these armies with devastating effect, winning a series of stunning victories, even if, at times, these victories had to be bolstered by his propaganda machine. 'Many faults, no doubt, will be found in my career,' he commented in 1820, 'but Arcole, Rivoli, the Pyramids, Marengo, Austerlitz, Jena, Friedland – these are granite: the tooth of envy is powerless here' (quoted in Herold, 1955: 274). The thrilling memory of these victories and of his tragic destiny, ending like the classical hero Prometheus bound to a rock in the ocean, had a profound impact on many young romantics of the early nineteenth century. Men like Alfred de Musset and Alfred de Vigny lamented that, reaching manhood during the Restoration they had somehow missed out on a glorious moment in history (*Doc. 19*). Such feelings were encapsulated by the novelist Stendhal in Julien Sorel, the tragic hero of *Le rouge et le noir*. But besides winning battles, Napoleon also over-reached himself by starting wars in countries where some men did not fight by either the old or the new rules, and where men did not seem to know when they appeared to be beaten. It is significant that his list of great victories quoted above, ends in 1807.

It is possible to assert that Napoleon aspired to creating a pacific and pacified, united states of Europe. Though it seems extremely doubtful that he ever possessed any long-term, considered plan for such. The musings and self-justifications on St Helena hardly hold up as serious proof of this aspiration. It is possible to argue over the extent to which Napoleon's wars were forced upon him, though the way in which war was seen to pay for itself and foster a spoils system for supporters tends to undermine the broad arguments of Napoleon's apologists in this respect. Moreover, his systematic humiliation of most of the most powerful crowned heads of Europe – first on the battlefield and then at the conference table – was never going to ensure their acceptance of him as a friendly neighbour or a permanent ally. No doubt Napoleon will continue to have those who are for him and those who are against. There is evidence for the partisans of both sides, but collecting evidence to prove a predetermined case ought not to be the aim of the historian.

PART FOUR   DOCUMENTS

Laure, Duchesse d'Abrantès (1784–1838) was the wife of General Junot. She had been educated in her mother's salon, a popular venue during the Directory, and had known Napoleon since her youth. In her lively, gossipy memoirs she describes his reception in Paris after his first Italian campaign. The law of the maximum was a system of price controls advocated by radical Jacobins particularly during the Terror.

However great Napoleon's vanity, it must have been well satisfied, for, as I have said, all classes united to welcome him on his return home. The people cried: 'Long live General Bonaparte!', 'Long live the conqueror of Italy!', 'Long live the peace-maker of Campo Formio!'. The bourgeoisie said: 'May God preserve him, for the sake of our glory and for delivering us from the law of the maximum and the Directory!' The upper class, now ungagged and released from their chains, ran with enthusiasm towards a young man who in a year had passed from the battle of Montenotte to the Treaty of Leoben, from victory to victory. Since then it has become possible to see his faults, even serious ones, but during that epoch he was seen as a pure and mighty colossus of glory. All the authorities provided magnificent fêtes for him; the Directory appeared in all its ludicrous pomp, including cloaks and plumed hats. ... While the fêtes were splendid in themselves, they possessed the added charm of celebrating the restoration to us of what we thought we had lost. Money began to circulate again, and the result of it was that everyone was content.

Laure, Duchesse d'Abrantès, *Mémoires*, Paris, 1831, vol. II, pp. 123–4. Quoted in
D.G. Wright, *Napoleon and Europe*, London: Longman, 1984, pp. 99–100.

Louis Antoine Henri de Bourbon Condé, the Duc d'Enghien (1772–1804) was the son of the Prince of Condé. He served with the emigré armies during the Revolutionary Wars but, with the Peace of Lunéville (1801) he married and retired to Ettenheim in Baden. Early in 1804 Napoleon was informed of a royalist plot that was supposed to be sparked by the arrival of a Bourbon prince in France. In consequence French gendarmes crossed into Baden and seized d'Enghien. He was taken to the fortress of Vincennes, tried by a drumhead court martial and shot. Fouché, Minister of Police, was uninvolved with the arrest and execution. The case of Madame Doux illustrates how the police attempted to keep abreast of public opinion and respond to even relatively minor incidents of sedition.

(a) From Fouché's recollections

I was one of the first to know of the mission of Caulaincourt and of Ordener to the banks of the Rhine; but when I knew that the telegraph announced the arrest of the prince and that the order had been given to transfer him from Strasbourg to Paris, I feared the catastrophe and I trembled for the noble victim. I hastened to Malmaison where the First Consul was staying; it was 29 *ventôse* (20 March 1804). I arrived there at nine o'clock in the morning, and I found him fidgety, walking alone in the park. I requested an interview on the great event of the day. 'I know what has brought you,' he said; 'today I will strike a great, but necessary blow.' I told him that he would incense France and Europe if he did not produce incontestable proof that the Duke had conspired against him in Ettenheim. 'What need of proof?' he shouted, 'isn't he a Bourbon, and the most dangerous of all of them?' I insisted on outlining the clear political reasons for maintaining silence about reasons of State. But it was in vain. He finished by saying to me with a smile: 'You and your like, haven't you said to me a hundred times that I would end up being the Monck of France and by re-establishing the Bourbons? Well! There's no going back. What stronger guarantee can I give to the Revolution that you cemented with the blood of a king? It's necessary to bring it to an end. I'm surrounded by conspiracies. It's necessary to imprint terror or to perish.'…

The indignation that I had foreseen erupted in the strongest fashion. I was one who dared to speak with thought on this offence against the law of nations and humanity. 'This was more than a crime,' I said, 'it is an error!' I report these words because they have been repeated and attributed to others.

Louis Madelin (ed.), *Les mémoires de Fouché*, Paris: Flammarion, 1945, pp. 215–17.

(b) Report from *commissaire de police* Pons of the Section Butte des Moulins to the Prefect of Police, 3 *Germinal* Year XII (24 March 1804)

You will see from the attached report from the commander of the [police] post in the rue du Lycée that the said Marie Geneviève Doux, living at 199 rue du Petit Reposoir, was arrested at the Palace of the Tribunal and sent to the said post for lack of a guard; and while at the post she dared to utter words against the First Consul and the army, saying notably that the troops in the post were involved in George's [Cadoudal's] conspiracy, that Bonaparte would not be where he was for long, and that she (the said Doux) would wish to have taken the place of the duc d'Enghien who had been a victim like Louis XVI.

When a person utters such words while drunk, it can be assumed that they indicate her way of thinking when sober. After this I have not thought,

Citizen Prefect, that the state of drunkenness in which, according to the report, the said Doux was found can excuse her conduct; for this reason I am sending her to you so that you may take such measures as you think fit.

Archives de la Préfecture de Police, A a/120, f.13.

DOCUMENT 3 THE POLICE STATE

The execution of the duc d'Enghien was a particularly extreme instance of political repression. As a rule the Napoleonic police state did not behave in such a manner. However, as the following documents show, it maintained a strict censorship of the press and the theatre, it kept suspect persons under surveillance, and it watched and listened to what was being done and what was being said with reference to the regime and its activities.

(a) To Fouché, 15 *Germinal* Year VIII (15 April 1800)

The intention of the Consuls of the Republic, Citizen Minister, is that the journals *Le Bien informé, Hommes libres* and *Défenseurs de la Patrie* shall cease publication, unless the proprietors find editors whose morality and patriotism is not sheltering corruption. You will ensure that each edition of these journals is signed by a recognised editor.

You will direct the Prefect of Police to take measures necessary

(1) to prevent bill-sticking on the walls of Paris, and any crying of journals and pamphlets without a police licence;
(2) to prevent print sellers from displaying for sale anything contrary to good morals and the principles of government.

The Prefect of Police will forbid the public announcement of any play unless the theatre director has a permit from the Minister of the Interior.

The Consuls wish you to send them, within the *décadi*, a report:

(1) on the best measures to rid Paris of the great number of Italian and other refugees who are here without any means of subsistence;
(2) on the measures you think appropriate to remove from the territory of the Republic those *émigrés* who have returned to the department of the Seine, whether or not they are under surveillance, unless they requested removal from the proscription list before 4 *Nivôse* last;
(3) on the names and addresses of around 50 individuals who, accustomed to living on the backs of revolutionary movements, are continually exciting public opinion; and on the best means of ridding Paris of these men, many of who are in foreign pay, play all kinds of role, and are available to those who will pay them to trouble the public peace.

Finally, you will make known to M. Payne* that the police have been informed of his suspect behaviour, and that on the first complaint against him, he will be sent back to his own country, America.

Bonaparte.

Cor[respondence de] Nap[oléon I], 32 vols, Paris, 1854–69, VI, no. 4707

(b) Report of the Prefect of Police, 15 February 1808

The crowd continues to visit the painting of *le Sacre* [David's painting of Napoleon's coronation]. At 12.30 p.m. on 14 February it was immense. Thirty students of David have entered the enclosure that separates the painting from the public, and have surrounded it with crowns. The spectators have shared their enthusiasm, and cries of *Vive l'Empereur* are heard on all sides.

Ernest d'Hautrive (ed.), *La Police Secrète du Premier Empire: Bulletins quotidiens addressés par Fouché à l'Empereur 1808–1809*, Paris: Clavreuil, vol. 4 (1963), p. 63.

(c) Police Bulletin, Fouché to Napoleon, 13 and 14 March 1808

Paris ... Today all minds are occupied with titles. The old noble families in the Faubourg Saint-Germain and the Faubourg Saint-Honoré, who joked much about the institution of the *Légion d'honneur*, are not laughing today about the creation of titles; they begin to perceive that we can do without them; that beginning of the nobility of the reigning dynasty will be the tomb of their [dynasty]; that they can do no better than to try to link themselves with the new titles. The poor, obscure nobility is very discontented; it fears being left as bourgeois. Anglomaniacs dislike the new nobility ... they say that the old will re-establish itself and that the new nobles, who have insufficient fortune to perpetuate themselves, will be extinguished little by little. Parisian shopkeepers fear being scorned by the new nobility as they were by the old. Opinion needs to be enlightened about this institution to understand the intentions. The minister has dictated some notes for journal articles. Foreigners find that the new decrees that establish the nobility show more and more the power of the Emperor.

d'Hauterive (ed.), *La Police Secrète ... 1808–1809*, vol. 4, pp. 96–7.

---

* Tom Paine (1737–1809) Born in England, but became a leading pamphleteer for the colonists during the American War of Independence; returned to England where he wrote the radical pamphlet *The Rights of Man* (1791–92); fled to France; imprisoned during the Terror.

(d) Police Bulletin, Fouché to Napoleon, 21 December 1809

Paris. Today all classes of society speak of nothing other than the dissolution of the Emperor's marriage. The pious, the factious and women aged between 40 and 50 years disapprove of this action. ... The Dutch who are in Paris are showing considerable discontent about the bringing together of their country with France. They say that execution of the Emperor's decrees on the blockade will ruin Holland.

d'Hauterive (ed.), *La Police Secrète ... 1809–1810*, vol. 5 (1964), p. 272.

DOCUMENT 4   **THE CONCORDAT**

The Concordat was designed to heal the breach between the French State and the Catholic Church. The First Consul saw it as a means of disassociating the Church from the royalist opposition to his regime and hence weakening that opposition. The Concordat ensured the ultimate authority of the State over the Church in France. The Organic Articles, which were prepared without the Pope's approval, reinforced this authority. Friction between the Pope and Napoleon was to continue, however, resulting in the annexation of the Papal States, the arrest of the Pope, and the excommunication of Napoleon. The Concordat of Fontainebleau designed to restore peace once again, was forced upon the Pope in 1813, but, almost immediately, he repudiated his signature.

(a) The Concordat, signed 23 *Fructidor* Year XI (10 Sept. 1801), published Easter Sunday (8 April) 1802

The government of the republic acknowledges that the catholic religion, apostolic and Roman, is the religion of the great majority of French citizens.

His holiness also acknowledges that this religion has derived, and is likely to derive, the greatest advantages and lustre from the establishment of the catholic faith in France, and from the particular profession of it, by the consuls of the republic.

They, therefore, after this mutual acknowledgement, made as well for the interest of religion, as for the support of the internal tranquillity of their respective states, have agreed as follows:

Article I. The catholic religion, apostolic and Roman, shall be freely exercised in France. Its worship shall be public, but in conformity to such regulations of police as government shall judge necessary for the public tranquillity.

II. There shall be made by the holy see, in concert with the government, a new division of French dioceses.

III. His holiness shall declare to those who have now the rank of French bishops, that he confidently expects from them all manner of sacrifices, even that of their sees, for the sake of peace and unity. After this exhortation, if they shall refuse to make this sacrifice, that the interest of the church requires (a refusal, which, however, his holiness does not expect), other persons shall be provided for the government of the bishoprics, constituted by the new division of sees, in the following manner:

IV. The first consul of the republic shall name, within three months after the publication of his holiness's bull, to the archbishoprics and bishoprics of the new division, his holiness will confer the canonical institution according to the forms established with regard to France before the change of its government.

V. The nomination to the bishoprics which shall afterwards become vacant, shall be also made by the first consul; and the canonical institution shall be confirmed by the holy see as in the foregoing article.

VI. The bishops, before they enter upon their functions, shall take, before the first consul, in person, the oath of fidelity, which was in use before the change of government, expressed in the following terms: 'I swear and promise to God, upon the holy evangelists, to preserve obedience and fidelity to the government established by the constitution of the French republic. I also promise to have no correspondence, nor to assist at any council or cabal, either within the country or out of it, that shall be contrary to the cause of the public tranquillity; and if in my diocese, or elsewhere, I shall learn of any plots or machinations prejudicial to the state, I shall inform the government of it.'

VII. The clergy of the second order shall take the same oath before the civil authorities appointed by the government.

VIII. The following prayer shall be recited at the end of divine service in all the catholic churches of France:

Domine, salvam fac rempublicum!
Domino, salvos fac consules!

IX. The bishops shall make a new division of parishes in their dioceses. Which shall, however, not be conclusive, till it has received the consent of the government.

X. The bishops shall name the curés. Their choice must, however, be agreed by the government.

XI. The bishops may have a chapter in their cathedral, and a seminary for their diocese, without the government being bound to endow them.

XII. All the metropolitan, cathedral, parochial, and other churches, that have not yet been disposed of, shall be placed at the disposition of the bishop.

XIII. His holiness, for the cause of peace, and the happy re-establishment of the catholic religion, declares, that neither he nor his successors shall trouble in any manner the acquirers of ecclesiastical property that has been alienated and that consequently the ownership of the said property together with all the revenues and rights attached in it, shall remain with the said acquirers, or those to whom they have transferred.

XIV. The government will secure a suitable provision for the bishops and curés whose diocese and parishes shall be marked out by the new divisions.

XV. The government shall take measures to permit those French catholics, who shall be so disposed, to form establishments and foundations in favour of the churches.

XVI. His holiness acknowledges in the first consul of the French republic the same rights and prerogatives which the ancient government possessed with him...

Annual Register, 1802, Public Papers, pp. 152–3.

(b) The Organic Articles

No bull, brief, etc. of the court of Rome shall have any effect in France without the consent of the government.

No individual, apostolic nuncio, legate, etc. shall be permitted to exercise their functions in France but with the consent of the government, and in a manner conformable to the liberties of the Gallican church.

No national council, or diocesan synod, shall take place without the consent of government.

The council of state shall take cognisance of disturbances caused by the ministers in the execution of their functions, or of other persons against them.

Bishops may add to their titles the qualification of *citoyen*, or *monsieur*.

No man can be named a bishop but a *Frenchman*, aged at least thirty years, having an attestation of his morals delivered by a bishop, and after an examination of his doctrine by a bishop and two priests.

Bishops may not quit their sees without the permission of the first consul.

The clergy in general shall wear black clothes, the bishops violet coloured stockings.

There shall be a liturgy and a catechism for the French church.

The new calendar, which begins at the autumnal equinox, is preserved. The names of the days shall be as in the ancient calendar. Sunday shall be the day of rest for the public functionaries.

There shall be ten archbishoprics and 50 bishoprics.

The allowance of the archbishop shall be 15,000 livres annually, of the bishops,10,000.

No clergyman shall be ordained as priest, who is not 25 years of age, and possessed of 300 livres annual revenue.

The curés shall reside in their parishes. Priests who do not regularly belong to any diocese, shall not officiate.

No other holidays, except Sundays, shall be kept without the consent of the government.

The bells shall only be rung for divine service.

The bishops shall visit every year a part of their diocese, the whole every five years.

No religious ceremony shall take place out of the temples in those towns, where there are temples dedicated to the different forms of worship. The same temple shall be consecrated only to one form of worship. The nuptial benedictions shall be only given by the clergy to those who have been married by the civil officers. ...

Annual Register, 1802, State Papers, p. 154.

(c) The Concordat of Fontainebleau, signed 25 January 1813

His majesty the Emperor and King and his Holiness being inclined to put an end to the differences which have arisen between them, and to provide against the difficulties that have taken place in several affairs concerning the church, have agreed upon the following articles, which are to serve as a basis for a definitive arrangement:

Article 1. His Holiness shall exercise the pontificate in France, and in the kingdom of Italy, in the same manner, and with the same forms as his predecessors.

...

Article 3. The domains which were possessed by the Holy Father, and that have not been alienated, shall be exempted from all kinds of imposts, and shall be administered by his agents or chargés d'affaires. Those which were alienated, shall be replaced, as far as to the amount of two million of francs in revenue.

Article 4. Within the space of six months following the notification of the usage of nomination by the emperor to the archbishoprics and bishoprics of the empire and the kingdom of Italy, the pope shall give the canonical investiture in conformity with the Concordat. ... The six months being expired without the pope having accorded the investiture, the metropolitan, or in default of him, where a metropolitan is in question, the oldest bishop in the province, shall proceed to the investiture of the new bishop, in such a manner that a see shall never be vacant longer than one year.

...

Article 10. His Majesty restores his good favour to those cardinals, bishops, priests and lay-brethren, who have incurred his displeasure in consequence of actual events.

The Holy Father agrees to the above dispositions, in consideration of the actual state of the church, and in the confidence with which his Majesty has inspired him, that he will grant his powerful protection to the numerous wants which religion suffers in the times we live in.

Annual Register, 1813, State Papers, pp. 389–90.

DOCUMENT 5   THE JEWS AND RELIGIOUS POLICY

The recollections that Napoleon gave of his life and intentions on St Helena have to be considered with the utmost care. The following is his explanation of his policies towards the Jews and of his attitude to religion within the State. Barry O'Meara was an Irish-born British naval surgeon who acted as Napoleon's physician on St Helena. His sympathy for Napoleon contributed to a feud with the governor, Sir Hudson Lowe, and led to him being expelled from the island.

During the conversation I took the liberty of asking the emperor his reasons for having encouraged the Jews so much. He replied, 'I wanted to make them leave off usury, and become like other men. There were a great many Jews in the countries I reigned over; by removing their disabilities, and by putting them upon an equality with Catholics, Protestants, and others, I hoped to make them become good citizens, and conduct themselves like the rest of the community. I believe that I should have succeeded in the end. My reasoning with them was, that, as their rabbins [sic] explained to them that they ought not to practise usury against their own tribes, but were allowed to practise it with Christians and others, that, therefore, as I had restored them to all their privileges, and made them equal to my other subjects, they must consider me, like Solomon or Herod, to be the head of their nation, and my subjects as brethren of a tribe similar to theirs. That, consequently, they were not permitted to deal usuriously with them or me, but to treat us as if we were of the tribe of Judah. That enjoying similar privileges to my other subjects, they were, in like manner, to pay taxes, and to submit to the laws of conscription, and to other laws. By this I gained many soldiers. Besides, I should have drawn great wealth to France, as the Jews are very numerous, and would have flocked to a country where they enjoyed such superior privileges. Moreover, I wanted to establish an universal liberty of conscience. My system was to have been no predominant religion, but to allow perfect liberty of conscience and of thought, to make all men equal, whether Protestants, Catholics, Mahometans, Deists or others; so that their religion should have no influence in getting them employments under governments. In fact, that it should neither be the means of serving, nor of injuring them; and that no objection should be made to a man's getting a situation on the score of religion, provided he were fit for it in other respects. I made everything independent of religion. All the tribunals were so. Marriages were independent of the priests; even the burying grounds were not left at their disposal, as they could not refuse interment to the body of any person, of whatsoever religion. My intention was to render every thing belonging to the state and the constitution, purely civil without reference to any religion. I wished to deprive the priests of all influence and power in civil affairs, and to oblige them to confine themselves to their own spiritual matters, and meddle with nothing else.'

Barry E. O'Meara, *Napoleon in Exile; or, A Voice from St. Helena*, 4th edn, 2 vols, London, 1822, I, pp. 182–4.

DOCUMENT 6   THE CODE NAPOLÉON

The Code civile des Français *was promulgated on 21 March 1804 and became officially known at the* Code Napoléon *from September 1807. The following extracts are designed to give a flavour of the paternalist nature of the document and some of the attitudes towards property.*

Book I Of Persons

Title 1 Of the Enjoyment and Privation of Civil Rights
Chapter I Of the Enjoyment of Civil Rights

7. The exercise of civil rights is independent of the quality of citizen, which is only acquired and preserved conformably to the constitutional law.
8. Every Frenchman shall enjoy civil rights.
9. Every individual born in France of a foreigner, may, during the year which shall succeed the period of his majority, claim the quality of Frenchman...

Title V Of Marriage
Chapter I Of the Qualities and Conditions required in order to be able to contract Marriage

144. A man before the age of 18, and a woman before 15 complete, are incapable of contracting marriage.
145. The government shall be at liberty nevertheless, upon weighty reasons, to grant dispensation of age.

...

148. The son who has not attained the full age of 25 years, the daughter who has not attained the full age of 21 years, cannot contract marriage without the consent of their father and mother; in case of disagreement, the consent of the father is sufficient.

149. If one of the two be dead, or under the incapacity of manifesting his or her will, the consent of the other is sufficient.

...

Chapter VI Of the respective Rights and Duties of Married Persons

212. Married persons owe to each other fidelity, succour, assistance.
213. The husband owes protection to his wife, the wife obedience to her husband.
214. The wife is obliged to live with her husband, and to follow him to every place where he may judge it convenient to reside: the husband is obliged to receive her, and to furnish her with every thing necessary for the wants of life, according to his means and station.
215. The wife cannot plead in her own name, without the authority of her husband, even though she be a public trader, or non-communicant, or separate in property.

...

217. A wife, although non-communicant or separate in property, cannot give, alienate, pledge, or acquire by free or chargeable title, without the concurrence of her husband in the act, or his consent in writing.

...

Title VI Of Divorce
Chapter I Of the Causes of Divorce

229. The husband may demand a divorce on the ground of his wife's adultery.
230. The wife may demand divorce on the ground of adultery in her husband when he shall have brought his concubine into their common residence.
231. The married parties may reciprocally demand divorce for outrageous conduct, ill-usage, or grievous injuries, exercised by one of them towards the other.

...

Title IX Of Paternal Power

371. A child, at every age, owes honour and respect to his father and mother.
372. He remains subject to their control until his majority or emancipation.
373. The father alone exercises this control during marriage.
374. A child cannot quit the paternal mansion without permission of his father unless for voluntary enlistment after the full age of eighteen years.
375. A father who shall have cause of grievous dissatisfaction at the conduct of a child, shall have the following means of correction.

376. If the child have not commenced his sixteenth year, the father may cause him to be confined for a period which shall not exceed one month. ...

377. From the age of sixteen years commenced to the majority or emancipation, the father is only empowered to require the confinement of his child during six months at the most...

378. There shall not be in either case, any writing or judicial formality, except the order itself for arrest, in which the reasons thereof shall not be set forth. The father shall only be required to subscribe an undertaking to defray all expenses and to supply suitable support.

379. The father is always at liberty to abridge the duration of the confinement...

...

Title XI Of Majority, Interdiction and the Judicial Adviser
Chapter I Of Majority

488. Majority is fixed at twenty-one years completed; at this age a person is capable of all acts regarding civil life, saving the restrictions contained under the title '*of Marriage*'.

Book II Of Property, and the Different Modifications of Property

Title I Of the Distinction of Property

...

Chapter III Of Property with Reference to those who are in Possession of it

537. Private persons have the free disposition of the property belonging to them, subject to the modifications established by the laws.

...

Title II Of Property

544. Property is the right of enjoying and disposing of things in the most absolute manner, provided they are not used in a way prohibited by the laws or statutes.

545. No one can be compelled to give up his property, except for the public good, and for a just and previous indemnity.

...

Book III Of the Different Modes of Acquiring Property

General Dispositions

711. Ownership in goods is acquired and transmitted by succession, by donation between living parties, or by will and by the effect of obligation.

Section III Of successions devolving upon Descendants

745. Children or their descendants succeed to their father and mother, grandfathers, grandmothers, or other ancestors, without distinction of sex or primogeniture, and although they be the issue of different marriages.

They succeed by equal portions and by heads. ...

...

Chapter IV Of Irregular Successions
Section I Of the Rights of Natural Children...

756. Natural children are not heirs; the law does not grant to such any rights over the property of their father or mother deceased, except where they have been legally recognised. ...

The Code Napoléon or, the Civil Code, literally translated from the original and official edition published at Paris, in 1804, By a Barrister of the Inner Temple, London, 1824.

DOCUMENT 7   **THE CONFEDERATION OF THE RHINE**

The Confederation of the Rhine was established by Napoleon in July 1806 in the expectation that it would develop into a unified body based upon French models. The Archbishop of Mainz, Karl Theodor von Dalberg, who shared these aspirations, was appointed Prince-Primate (Fürstenprimas). Among the principal members from the beginning were the Kings of Bavaria and Württemberg, the Grand Dukes of Baden, Berg, and Hesse-Darmstadt. They were later joined by the Kings of Saxony and Westphalia and other smaller principalities and dukedoms.

Article I. The states of the contracting princes ... shall be for ever separated from the German body, and united, by a particular confederation, under the designation of 'the confederated states of the empire'.

Article II. All the laws of the [German] empire, by which they have been hitherto bound, shall be in future null and without force. ...

Article III. Each of the contracting princes renounces such of his titles as refer to his connection with the German empire, and they will, on the first of August, declare their entire separation from it.

...

Article VI. The affairs of the confederation shall be discussed in a congress of the union (Diet) whose place of sitting shall be in Frankfort, and the congress shall be divided into two colleges, the kings and the princes.

Article VII. The members of the league must be independent of every foreign power. They cannot, in any wise, enter into any other service, but that of the states of the confederation and its allies. ...

...

Article XII. The emperor [Napoleon] shall be proclaimed protector of the confederation. On the demise of the primate [Dalberg] he shall, in such quality, as often name the successor.

...

Article XXXV. Between the emperor of the French and the confederated states ... there shall be an alliance, by virtue of which every continental war in which one or either of the parties shall be engaged shall be common to all.

Annual Register, 1806, State Papers, pp. 818–23.

DOCUMENT 8   PROBLEMS WITH CONSCRIPTION

Annual conscription was introduced by the loi Jourdan *of 1798. All men aged between 20 and 25 were liable for conscription. They were divided into classes according to their age, and the call up of classes depended on the military situation. The demands were particularly heavy in 1807 and 1808 and, above all, in 1813. Over the years, it would seem that conscription began to be accepted as a fact of life within France though a variety of methods of avoidance continued to be attempted. The incidence of riots and resistance seems to have decreased in France. But such a decrease was much less apparent within other territories of the Empire.*

(a) Gendarmerie report from Pamiers, Department of Ariège.

Today, 2 Thermidor Year XIII [21 July 1805] we, Nicolas Malhieu, *maréchal des logis* [sergeant], Michel Saucher, *brigadier* [corporal], accompanied by gendarmes Patrie, Geoffroy, Maury, Cathala and Toupet, ... having been advised that there was a large number of refractory conscripts in the commune of Segura, who were being aided by the mayors of Segura and Mailliou, we became convinced of it by the following events. ... In order to effect the arrest of some of these refractory conscripts, at the end of Mass [in Segura] ... we surrounded the church door. Here we arrested Pierre Thoux and Joseph Sabatien, who were both outside the door. As the service ended and the *curé* and the people came out, it became clear that they intended to impede our action. We entered the church to search for the conscripts who, we suspected, were hiding there. As a result of our search we found Antoine Sabatien, who told us that his name was Pierre Subatica and then that he was Pierre Fouta of Dalou, Jean Saury, of the commune of Buitenac, and Joseph, also of Buitenac, who refused to give us his surname. We asked the mayors of Segura and Malliou to show us the birth certificates of the men that we had arrested. We were not surprised by the mayors' response that they could not show us the birth certificates but that they would give us attestations that the arrested men were not in fact conscripts, we were already convinced that one of the conscripts had already been convicted and that these attestations would be false. We considered the mayors to be totally opposed to us; so too was the *curé*, who, referring to the gendarmes, declared in a loud voice that his church was the gathering place for robbers. We were resigned to leaving with just the seven refractory conscripts that we had arrested and bound with cords. But, seeing the storm that was gathering around us we were not surprised when, twenty paces from the church, we heard shouts of 'Get the wolves' and 'Get the robbers', and then we were attacked with stones. ... At least two hundred people, both men and women, assailed us and in the *mêlée* they cut the cords binding two of the conscripts that we had found under the church altar. In spite of our efforts, these two escaped. Seeing the people roused to such a fury, doubtless on the instructions of the mayors of Segura and Mailliou – who ought to have put on their sashes of office, restrained the people and helped to re-establish order – we gendarmes showed character and firmness and, in spite of the disorder, with skill we were able to escort five conscripts to Pamiers without striking anyone.

Archives Nationales, BB18 7.

(b) Marshal Moncey, Inspector General of the Gendarmerie, to Napoleon, 3 February 1806

On 27 January the Gendarmerie detachment at Courlay [Deux-Sèvres] arrested two refractory conscripts in a village in this arrondissement. The following day at 7.00 a.m. three gendarmes were directed to conduct them to Bressuire. But barely half way, as they entered the commune of Clazain, they met with a volley of forty or fifty shots and two gendarmes, Bourget, based at Argenton-Chateau, and Chatelain, based at Moncoutant, were killed. The third gendarme, seeing the assailants coming for him in considerable numbers, was forced to retire to avoid the same fate and to report the incident. [The Gendarmerie lieutenant at Bressuire] has learned that these rebels threw themselves furiously on gendarme Bourget, wounded by several shots but not yet dead, and finished him off by beating him to death with his own carbine. It seems that this attack was carried out by individuals from the Commune of Courlay who had prepared the ambush during the night. The lieutenant complains of the bad spirit to be found in this commune.

Archives Nationales, AF IV 1156.

(c) Police bulletin, Fouché to Napoleon, 8 May 1809

In the town of Toulon, following the rumour of a next call of conscripts from the later classes, there has been a resort to marriage as a means of avoidance. On 27 April the chief *commissaire* wrote that marriages had never been so numerous in this town.

d'Hauterive (ed.), *La Police Secrète ... 1809–1810*, vol. 5, p. 41.

(d) Police bulletin, Fouché to Napoleon, 16 October 1809

The Prefect of Gironde writes that, with the intention of hiding him from conscription, a father came to the mayor of his commune with the intention of registering as a *girl*, the *son* to whom his wife had just given birth. He notes that, within the existing laws, there is no sanction for this offence.

d'Hautrive (ed.), *La Police Secrète ... 1809–1810*, vol. 5, pp. 213–14.

(e) Police bulletin, Savary to Napoleon, 18 October 1811

A conscript [in Münster] has cut off his finger to avoid service. Questioned by the chief *commissaire* he said that a relative advised him to do this and carried out the amputation. The relation of the conscript is being sought; they are both the sons of artisans.

Nicole Gotteri (ed.), *La Police Secrète du Premier Empire: Bulletins quotidiens adressés par Savary à l'Empereur de juillet à décembre 1811*, Paris: Honoré Champion, 1991, vol. 3, p. 267.

DOCUMENT 9   **VISITING HIS TROOPS**

Private Danserville was a peasant boy from the countryside around Beauvais, due north of Paris, in the Department of Oise. His letter to his uncle from his base in northern Italy reveals the kind of excitement that a visit by the Emperor could generate within regiments.

At last we have enjoyed the presence of our Sovereign, which we had been promised for a long time; he inspected our Division at Palma-Nuova in the midst of rain, mud, and snow; I don't think I have ever been so cold as I was that day, and I don't know how the Emperor could bear it, since the soldiers were scarcely able to handle their weapons; but it seemed that his very presence warmed us, and repeated shouts of *Vive l'Empereur!* must have convinced him how much he is cherished. Time did not allow him to go through all the ranks; he spoke only to the officers, but those soldiers who wanted to say something to him could approach him with confidence, certain of a warm welcome.

Archives Départementales, Oise, R (non-classé), Private Danserville to his uncle, 20 Dec. 1807; quoted in Forrest, 2002, p. 103.

DOCUMENT 10   TRAINING A NEW ÉLITE: THE *AUDITEURS*

Napoleon was keen to develop a new administrative elite that would be free from nostalgia for the old regime and republican ideas from the Revolution. The Corps of Auditeurs, *which numbered up to 400 men, was his principal instrument here. The auditeurs were young men from good families, but who could also show administrative and intellectual abilities. They usually began their careers with a probationary period attached to a section of the* Conseil d'état *or to a ministry. They could then move on to be a subprefect or an official in a ministry or in one of the satellites, steadily rising through the hierarchy to finish as a prefect. In 1809 Napoleon outlined his thinking on the* auditeurs *to the* Conseil d'état *thus:*

The purpose of the institution is to bring under the Emperor's wing men of the élite who are sincerely devoted to him, who have sworn an oath between his hands, whom he will observe closely enough to appreciate their zeal and their talents. They will be formed, so to speak, in his school, and he will be able to employ them wherever the needs of his service will make them useful. From this will emerge veritable magistrates and administrators. ... His Majesty's intention is [also] that the *auditeurs* be received at court, so that if they are on the one hand trained in work, they will on the other hand develop urbanity, the good taste and usages of society, which are necessary in the places where they might be assigned.

Quoted in Woloch, 2001a: 173–4.

DOCUMENT 11   ADVICE AND REPRIMANDS FOR FAMILY MEMBERS

While not the eldest brother Napoleon saw himself as the head of the family and was free with advice for family members. While this advice could be generous and, possibly helpful, he never let his brothers forget that he was the head of the Empire, that they owed their thrones to him, and that they should therefore behave in accordance with his plans. The advice, however, as the letters to Louis and Jerome show, was never restricted to political matters.

(a)   Instructions to Prince Eugène Viceroy of Italy
      Milan, 7(?) June, 1805

By entrusting you with the government of our Kingdom of Italy, we have given you proof of the respect that your conduct has inspired in us. But you are still at an age when one is unaware of the perversity in human hearts, I cannot therefore recommend circumspection and prudence too strongly to you. Our Italian peoples are more deceitful by nature than the citizens of France. There is only one way that you can keep their respect and serve their happiness, and that is by letting no one have your complete confidence, and by never telling anyone what you really think of the ministers and high officials that surround you. ... The aim of your administration is the happiness of my Italian peoples; and the first sacrifice you will have to make will be to accept certain of their customs that you detest. In any position other than that of Viceroy of Italy you may glory in being a Frenchman: but here you must forget it, and you will only succeed if you persuade the Italians that you love them. They know there is no love without respect. Learn their language; frequent their society; single them out for particular attention at public ceremonies; approve what they approve and like what they like. ...

Don't imitate me in every respect; you need more reserve.

Don't often preside over the Council of State; you don't have sufficient experience to do so successfully. I see no problem in your attending it whilst an assessor acts as president from his ordinary seat. Your ignorance of Italian, and also of legislation, are excellent excuses for staying away. Never make a speech to the Council: they would listen to you without reply, but they would see at once that you aren't yet competent to discuss business. You cannot measure the power of a prince who keeps silent; when he speaks, he has to know his superior ability.

Don't trust spies. They are more trouble than they are worth. There is never enough unrest at Milan to bother about, and it's probably the same elsewhere. Your military police make sure of the army, and that is all you want.

The army is the one thing that can occupy you, using your own knowledge.

Work with your ministers twice a week: once with each of them separately, and once with them all together in Council. You will be well on the way when your ministers and councillors are convinced that your only object in consulting them is to listen to reason, and prevent yourself from being surprised. ...

There is only one essential man here, the minister of finance: he is a hard worker who knows his job well.

Although they know I am behind you, I don't doubt but that they are trying to assess your character. See that your orders are carried out, particularly in the army: never allow them to be disobeyed. ...

Write to me every day and tell me what you are doing. It is only by degrees that you will learn how I conceive of each question and each object.

Don't show my letters to anyone, under any pretext whatsoever. It should not be known what I write to you, nor even that I write. Keep a room to which no one is admitted, not even your private secretaries. ...

One last word. Punish dishonesty ruthlessly. The exposure of a dishonest accountant is a victory for the government. And don't allow any smuggling by the French army.

Cor. Nap., X, no. 8852.

(b)   To Louis, King of Holland
       Finkenstein, 4 April 1807

...You say that you have 20,000 men with the Grand Army. You don't really believe it. There are not 10,000 of them, and what men! It's not marshals, knights and counts we need, but soldiers. If you go on like this, you will become ridiculous in Holland. You govern this nation too much like a monk. The benevolence of a king should be majestic, not that of a monk. Nothing could be worse than all these journeys to the Hague, unless it is the enquiry that you have ordered in your kingdom. A king gives orders, he does not ask anything of anyone. He is supposed to be the fountain of all power, and to have sufficient means so that he never needs recourse to another's purse. But all of these nuances are beyond you.

I recall some notions of re-establishing the nobility, but I remain unclear about them. Have you lost your head over this point, and forgotten your obligations to me? Your letters are always talking of respect and obedience; I don't want words but deeds. Respect and obedience consist in not going so fast in such important matters without my advice; Europe cannot imagine that you are so lacking in regard as to act without my advice. I shall be obliged to disown you. ... You must expect some public expression of my severe displeasure. ...

Your quarrels with the queen are also becoming public. If only you would keep for your family life the paternal and effeminate character that you exhibit in government, and apply to public affairs the rigour that you display at home! You treat a young wife as you would a regiment. ...

Cor. Nap., XV, no. 12294.

(c)   To Jerome, King of Westphalia
       Fontainebleau, 15 November 1807

You will find enclosed the Constitution for your kingdom. This Constitution contains the conditions by which I renounce all rights of conquest and all rights acquired over your kingdom. You must observe it faithfully. The happiness of your people is important to me, not only because of the influence it can have on your reputation and mine, but also from the point of view of the general system of Europe. Refuse to listen to those who tell you that your people, accustomed to servitude, will receive the benefits you bring them with ingratitude. They are more enlightened in the Kingdom of Westphalia than some would have you believe; and your throne will only become truly established through the confidence and affection of the people. What the peoples of Germany impatiently desire is that men who are not nobles but who have talent will have an equal claim to your consideration and to employment; they also want the total abolition of servitude and all intermediate links between the sovereign and the lowest class of people. The benefits of the Code Napoléon, public trials, the introduction of juries, will be the distinctive characteristics of your monarchy. ... It is necessary for your subjects to enjoy a liberty, an equality and a well-being hitherto un-known among the peoples of Germany, and that your liberal government produces, one way or another, changes which will be most salutary for the Confederation [of the Rhine] and for the strength of your monarchy. This way of governing will prove a more powerful barrier separating you from Prussia than the Elbe, the fortresses and the protection of France. What people will wish to return to the arbitrary government of Prussia when they have tasted the benefits of wise and liberal administration? The peoples of Germany, as well as those of France, Italy and Spain, desire equality and demand liberal ideas. I have been managing the affairs of Europe long enough to be convinced that the droning of the privileged is contrary to the wishes of general opinion. Be a constitutional king. When reason and the thinkers of your era are insufficient, good policy will instruct you in your position. You will find yourself with a power of opinion and a natural ascendancy over your neighbours who are absolutist kings.

Cor. Nap., XVI, no. 13361.

(d)   To Jerome,
       Paris, 6 March 1808

... I have seen few men with so little sense of proportion as you. You know nothing, yet you let your head lead you; you decide nothing by reason, but everything by impulse and passion. I only wish to correspond with you concerning indispensable matters relating to foreign courts, since here you take steps and expose your disagreements with me before the eyes of Europe: and that's something I am not prepared to allow. As for your internal and financial affairs, I repeat, as I said before, that nothing you do conforms to my opinions or my experience: and if you go on like this you will get nowhere. That said, I should be obliged if you would show a little less pomp and ostentation in procedures whose consequences you fail to appreciate. ...

Léon Lecestre (ed.), *Lettres inédites de Napoléon I*, 2 vols, Paris, 1897, I, no. 237.

DOCUMENT 12   ECONOMIC POLICY AND FRANCE

The economic system that Napoleon sought to establish within his Empire put France at the centre. The intention is clearly outlined in Napoleon's response to a request from Prince Eugène on behalf of the silk producers of the kingdom of Italy.

Saint-Cloud, 23 August 1810

My son,

I have received your letter of 14 August. All the raw silk from the kingdom of Italy goes to England, since no-one makes silk in Germany; therefore it is quite natural that I should wish to divert it from this route to the advantage of my French manufacturers; otherwise my silk factories, which constitute a principal resource of French commerce, would suffer substantial losses. I cannot agree with your observations. My principle is: *France first*. You must never lose sight of the fact that, if English commerce triumphs at sea, it is because the English are strongest there; it is therefore to be expected that, as France is strongest on land, she should claim commercial supremacy there; otherwise, all is lost. Isn't it better for Italy to come to the aid of France in such an important matter as this, rather than be covered in Customs Houses? For it would be short-sighted not to recognise that Italy is only independent because of France; that this independence was won by French blood and French victories, and that Italy must not abuse any of this; and that nothing could be more unreasonable than to start calculating what commercial advantages France gets out of it.

Piedmont and Parma produce silk too; and here I have prohibited its export to any country other than France. Why should Piedmont be treated in one way and the kingdom of Italy in another? If any discrimination were made, it should be in favour of Piedmont; for, while the Venetians fought against France, the Piedmontese came to her aid, they even took sides against their own king. But never mind all that. I understand Italian affairs better than anyone else. Italy cannot make calculations that leave French prosperity out of the account; she must recognise that the interests of the two countries are the same; above all, she must take care not to give France any reason for annexing her; for if this was in the interest of France, who could stop her? So make this your motto too – France first.

Cor. Nap., XXI, no.16824.

DOCUMENT 13   ECONOMIC WAR

In seeking to undermine British commerce to compel her to sue for peace, Napoleon was continuing a policy begun during the wars of the French Revolution. Under Napoleon, however, the policy reached a new level of intensity and tit-for-tat response. The following three documents constitute the best-known decrees relating to this aspect of the wars, and clearly illustrate the way that each side blamed the other for initiating the economic conflict and for involving neutrals.

(a) The imperial camp at Berlin, 21 November 1806

Napoleon, emperor of the French and king of Italy, etc., considering:

(1)   that England does not recognise the law of nations (*droit des gens*) universally followed by all civilised peoples;

(2)   that she considers as an enemy any individual belonging to the enemy's state, and consequently makes prisoners of war not only the crews of armed ships of war, but also the crews of commercial ships and merchant ships, and even commercial agents and merchants travelling on business;

(3)   that she extends the right of conquest, only applicable to that which belongs to an enemy state, to ships and commercial merchandise, and to the property of private individuals;

(4)   that she extends the right of blockade, which in accordance with reason and the customs of all civilised peoples is only applicable to fortified towns, to unfortified towns and commercial ports; that she declares in a state of blockade places before which she has not even a single ship of war ... that she even declares in a state of blockade places which all her united forces would be incapable of blockading...;

(5)   that this monstrous abuse of the right of blockade has no other aim than to prevent communication among peoples, and to raise the commerce and industry of England on the ruin of the commerce and industry of the continent;

(6)   that, since this is the clear aim of England, whoever deals on the continent in English goods is thereby favouring her designs, and renders himself her accomplice;

...

(8)   that it is a natural right to oppose the enemy with those arms that it employs...

We have resolved to apply to England the practices that she has consecrated in her maritime legislation.

The provisions of the present decree will be constantly considered as the fundamental principle of the Empire until England has recognised that the right of war is the same on land as on sea; that it cannot be extended either to private property ... or to the persons of individuals foreign to the profession of arms, and that the right of blockade should be restricted to fortified places properly besieged by sufficient forces.

We have consequently decreed and do decree the following:

Article 1. The British Isles are declared to be in a state of blockade.

Article 2. All commerce and all correspondence with the British Isles is forbidden. ...

Article 3. Every individual English subject ... who is found in any country occupied by our troops or by those of our allies, shall be made a prisoner of war.

Article 4. All warehouses, merchandise, property, of whatever kind, belonging to an English subject shall be considered a lawful prize.

Article 5. Trade in English merchandise is prohibited, and all goods belonging to England, or coming from her factories or her colonies, are declared lawful prizes.

Article 6. Half of the proceeds of the confiscation of merchandise and property declared lawful prizes by the preceding articles shall be used to indemnify merchants for losses experienced through the seizure of merchant ships by English cruisers.

Article 7. No vessel coming directly from England or from the English colonies, or having visited these since the publication of this decree, shall be received in any port.

Article 8. Any vessel which, by means of a false declaration, contravenes the above provisions, shall be seized. ...

...

Article 10. The present decree is to be communicated by our minister of foreign affairs to the Kings of Spain, Naples, Holland and Etruria, and to our other allies whose subjects, like ours, are the victims of the injustice and the barbarity of English maritime legislation. ...

Cor. Nap., XIII, no. 11,283.

(b) British Order in Council

At the Court at the Queen's Palace, January 7, 1807
Present, The King's Most Excellent Majesty in Council

Whereas the French government has issued certain orders, which, in violation of the usages of war, purport to prohibit the commerce of all neutral nations with his majesty's dominions; and also to prevent such nations from trading with any other country in any articles the growth, produce, or manufacture of his majesty's dominions; and whereas the said government has also taken upon itself to declare all his majesty's dominions in a state of blockade, at a time when the fleets of France and her allies are themselves confined within their own ports, by the superior valour and discipline of the British navy; and whereas such attempts on the part of the enemy would give to his majesty an unquestionable right of retaliation, and would warrant his majesty in enforcing the same prohibition of all commerce with France, which that power vainly hopes to effect against the commerce of his majesty's subjects, a prohibition which the superiority of his majesty's naval forces might enable him to support, by actually investing the ports and coasts of the enemy with numerous squadrons of cruizers, so as to make the entrance or approach thereto manifestly dangerous; and whereas his majesty, though unwilling to follow the example of his enemies, by proceeding to an extremity so distressing to all nations not engaged in the war, and carrying on their accustomed trade, yet feels himself bound by a due regard to the just defence of the rights and interests of his people, not to suffer such measures to be taken by the enemy, without taking some steps on his part to restrain this violence, and to retort upon them the evils of their own injustice; his majesty is thereupon pleased ... to order ... that no vessel shall be permitted to trade from one port to another, both of which ports shall belong to, or be in the possession of France or her allies, or shall be so far under their controul as that British vessels may not freely trade thereat; and the commanders of his majesty's ships of war and privateers ... are hereby instructed to warn every neutral vessel coming from any such port, and destined to another such port, to discontinue her voyage, and not to proceed to any such port; and any vessel, after being so warned, or any vessel coming from any such port, after a reasonable time shall have been afforded for receiving information of this his majesty's orders which shall be found proceeding to another such port, shall be captured and brought in, and, together with her cargo, shall be condemned as lawful prize. ...

Annual Register,1807, State Papers, pp. 671–2.

The above was strengthened by a new Order in Council on 11 November 1807, and this prompted the following:

(c) At our Royal Palace, at Milan, December 17, 1807

Napoleon, emperor of the French, king of Italy, and protector of the Rhenish Confederation:

Observing the measures adopted by the British government ... by which vessels belonging to neutral friendly, or even powers of the allies of England, are made liable, not only to be searched by English cruizers, but to be compulsorily detained in England, and to have a tax laid on them ...

Observing that by these acts the British government *denationalises* ships of every nation in Europe. ... We have decreed...

Article 1. Every ship, to whatever nation it may belong, that shall have submitted to be searched by an English ship, or to a voyage to England, or shall have paid any tax whatever to the English government, is thereby, and for that alone, declared to be *denationalised*, to have forfeited the protection of its king, and to have become English property.

Article 2. Whether the ships thus *denationalised* by the arbitrary measures of the English government, enter into our ports, or those of our allies, or whether they fall into the hands of our ships of war, or our privateers, they are declared to be good and lawful prizes.

Article 3. The British Isles are declared to be in a state of blockade both by land and sea. ...

Article 4. These measures, which are resorted to only in just retaliation of the barbarous system adopted by England, which assimilates its legislation to that of Algiers ... shall continue to be rigorously in force as long as that government does not return to the principle of the law of nations, which regulates the relations of civilised states in a state of war. ...

Annual Register, 1807, State Papers, pp. 779–80.

DOCUMENT 14   **PROBLEMS IN ENFORCING CUSTOMS DUTIES, TAXES AND THE BLOCKADE**

Increasing taxes and the implementation of the blockade against Britain were among the most unpopular elements of the Napoleonic regime. The trafficking in permitted goods without paying the appropriate duties (fraude) *and the smuggling of prohibited goods* (contrabande) *became major problems for the authorities, and all kinds of individual were involved.*

(a) Subprefect of Altkirch to Prefect of Haut-Rhin, 18 Fructidor Year XIII (5 September 1805)

Unfortunately it is only too true that smuggling is conducted to a degree frightening for the interests of our manufacturers and those of the public treasury. ... Public opinion indicates many individuals, even public officials, who must be engaged in it or else protecting it; it can be said that both the high and the low are mixed up in it; the latter are involved by the lure of gain, which the principal actors provide by paying generously for the trafficking that is usually done by night.

Archives Départementales, Haut-Rhin, P 295; French version quoted in Ellis, 1981, p. 205.

(b) Letter from the mayor (*podestà*) of Budrio, department of Reno, 25 June 1809

This morning I was shaken out of my sleep ... and [after] getting up I saw to my surprise that many people besieged my house and asked to enter and speak with me. [There were] three hundred and fifty individuals, almost all farmers. ... [They told me] that they did not want to bear the intolerable increase in consumption tax ... and especially the grain tax, and that no community of this vast country wants to be subjected to such a yoke; and that the inhabitants of all the neighbouring communities are united to start a rebellion if such unbearable weight becomes effective, since they are in such a distress that they cannot even find the money to pay the milling fees. ... I tried with all the possible means to calm them down, stating their needed obedience to the laws, and that they were subjects of a very powerful king who ruled over the whole of Europe ... that the immense needs of the war require resources and that when peace is achieved the burdens will diminish. ... But those are uncivil and uneducated people [who] are mostly poor ... [and hence] nothing served to calm their initial effervescence; they responded firmly and unanimously that they did not want to pay [the tax] or pick up the [tax] receipt, and that they will remove the weighing scale of the tax collectors, will show up armed at the mills and if the millers refuse to grind the wheat, they will grind it by themselves and will leave the usual amount of flour as a payment and nothing more.

Archivio di Stato di Bologna, CS, b.1, f. 17, quoted in Grab, 1995a, pp. 55–6.

(c) Police bulletin, Fouché to Napoleon, 28 October 1809

In a letter dated 25 of this month the Prefect of the Seine reports that, on the night of 5 of this month, 15 *fraudeurs*, men and women, forced the tollgate at La Villette in spite of the resistance of the agents and the 2 gendarmes who were requested to assist them. On 18th, around 10.00 p.m., another assembly of around 20 unknown individuals insulted and mistreated the employees at the tollgate of Saint Denis; three of the latter were seriously wounded. During the trouble at this tollgate, a great number of other men and women got through that of La Villette with bladders full of alcohol, insulting and threatening the employees who were too few in number to be able to stop them. The directors of the *octroi* have given instructions to use the greatest moderation so as not to excite trouble. The prefect has approved. He notes, however, that it is possible for these gatherings, under the pretext of *fraude*, to be directed by hidden hands that are intent on exciting trouble. Some of the words of the individuals in the crowds give rise to this suspicion. 'We only want to earn a living. Our profession is to be smugglers (*passeurs*) when there is no work for our trades. You've got to live and feed the children etc. etc.'

Consequently, the agents who oppose them become rogues. The Prefect of Police has been instructed to get information on the circumstances, to investigate the individuals involved in *fraude*, and to indicate the way to stop these disorders. Two police officers have been posted at the tollgates.

d'Hautrive (ed.), La Police Secrète ... 1809–1810, vol. 5, pp. 222–3.

(d) Police bulletin, Savary to Napoleon, 28 July 1810

On 9 March last *brigadier* Lefèvre and 4 gendarmes from Livorno were surprised fraudulently trafficking cocoa. Marshal, the duc de Conegliano [Moncey] was requested to issue orders for them to be taken before a competent tribunal and judged according to the law. By a letter of 16 July the chief *commissaire de police* at Livorno informs me that the judicial proceedings have not taken place. We must be content with these gendarmes being sent to other residences. The *brigadier* has been promoted to *maréchal des logis* and placed at San Marcello (Arno). – On 12 July the bishop of Livorno went out in his carriage by the Pisa gate and visited a new baths. During his visit the customs men searched his carriage and found five shoddy pieces of printed calico under the coachman's seat. They took possession of the carriage and its horses, putting it under the guard of one of their number in a neighbouring shed. When the bishop reappeared, the inspector and the controller led him to a separate building to interrogate him and take a statement. Some time afterwards, the prefect and the Director of the Customs arrived and returned the carriage to the bishop, who was driven back to his residence by a different coachman. This incident encouraged a numerous crowd to assemble, but public order was not threatened.

Gotteri (ed.), La Police Secrète ... juin à décembre 1810, vol. 1, p. 167.

(e) Police bulletin, Savary to Napoleon, 27 December 1811

The Gendarmerie reports that, on 12th of this month in the village of Milte near Osnabrück, Lieutenant Collin of the customs and one of his men surprised a wagon escorted by a score of armed individuals and loaded with bundles of wool and such fabrics. They attempted to seize it. The smugglers said that they would carry on in spite of them and, at the same moment, opened fire. Lieutenant Collin was hit in the thigh with a musket ball. But in spite of his wound, he responded like a customs man. They killed one of the smugglers; the others retired with their wagon. The next day 20 of the bundles were found near a house whose owner declared that they had been left there the night before by 6 individuals from Lasenberg in the Grand Duchy of Berg. The driver of the wagon was found to be a peasant of Milte named Gansopolh. He has been arrested.

Gotteri (ed.), La Police Secrète ... de juillet à décembre 1811, vol. 3, p. 430.

DOCUMENT 15 GENERAL MALET'S CONSPIRACY 1812

Claude-François de Malet (1754–1812) was born into the minor nobility and served briefly in the army during the old regime. He returned to the army during the Revolution, became a staunch republican and rose to the rank of general. Following an abortive coup in 1808 Malet was held in preventive detention. He escaped towards the end of 1812 and attempted a second coup proclaiming Napoleon's death in Russia and a restoration of the republic. The coup failed and Malet was shot.

To citizens and to the army

Bonaparte is no more! The tyrant has fallen under the blow of humanity's avengers. Give them thanks. On behalf of the motherland and the human race, they have well deserved it.

If we are ashamed about supporting a stranger, a Corsican, at our head for so long, we are too proud to suffer a bastard child in the same place. It is, therefore, our most sacred duty to support the Senate in its magnanimous resolution to free us of all tyrannies.

A sincere and ardent love of the motherland will inspire us with the means to see through this urgent and final revolution; but it is through your courage, your perfect union, your reciprocal confidence that we shall achieve a glorious success.

Citizens, on this never to be forgotten day, seize back all your spirit and rip out the shame of a base slavery. Honour and interest reunify themselves for you in making the law. There is a repressive regime to overturn; there is liberty to restore, never to lose it again. Strike down all that dare to oppose the national will; protect all that submit to it.

Soldiers, the same things should motivate you. There is an even more pressing matter for you: cease being prodigal with your blood in wars that are unjust, atrocious, interminable and against national independence. Prove to France, to Europe, that you will no more be the soldiers of Bonaparte than you were of Robespierre. You are and always will be the soldiers of the motherland, and she will restore to you the just rewards for your services that you have been deprived of for so long.

Legionnaires, civil and military, our institution [the *Légion d'honneur*] will be preserved. Don't doubt it, we owe this distinguished ribbon to the oath that we have made to defend Liberty, Equality and to combat Feudalism with all our might. Such is our oath. It should be engraved on our hearts...

Jean Burnat, G.H. Dumont and Émile Wanty (eds.), *Le dossier Napoléon*, Verviers: Éditions Gerard, 1962, pp. 218–19.

DOCUMENT 16   **THE RETREAT FROM MOSCOW**

Napoleon's Russian campaign was one of the greatest military disasters. Napoleon crossed the River Nieman and entered Russia at the head of around 600,000 men in June 1812. He fought an inconclusive battle at Borodino (7 September) and pressed on to Moscow, the Russians withdrawing before him. He entered an all but deserted Moscow on 14 September. The Russians refused to negotiate and after fires were started in the city the French began a withdrawal on 19 October. The battle of Maloyaroslaverts forced Napoleon to follow the same route back by which he had invaded. In November there were terrible frosts. At the end of the month the army crossed the River Berezina on pontoon bridges under fierce attack from the Russians. Napoleon left the remnants of his army for Paris on 5 December. On 18 December the remains of the army, about 18,000 men, crossed the Nieman.

(a) *From the recollections of Heinrich August Vossler who served as a lieutenant in one of the Württemberg Cavalry Regiments attached to the Grand Army during the Russian Campaign.*

The longer the retreat continued, the more ghastly became the sight of the fugitives. In the most frightful cold men could be seen toiling along the road without fur or overcoat, dressed only in a light suit, the frost visibly over-powering them. Their limbs gradually stiffened, they fell, picked themselves up painfully, staggered on a few paces, and fell once more never to rise again. Lack of sound and suitable footwear cost thousands of their lives. Some showed their naked toes through torn shoes or boots, first purple, then frozen dark blue or brown, and finally black. Others had wrapped their feet in rags, scraps of leather, furs or skins, which preserved their toes provided they could find replacements when the original covering wore out. Of those who were lucky enough to survive, thousands lost hands, feet, noses and ears from the frost. In many cases extremities simply broke off, in others fingers and toes, and often whole arms and legs, had to be amputated.

The ravages of cold were equalled by those of hunger. No food was so rotten or disgusting as not to find someone to relish it. No fallen horse or cattle remained uneaten, no dog, no cat, no carrion, nor, indeed, the corpses of those that died of cold or hunger. It was not unknown even for men to gnaw at their own famished bodies. But not only men's bodies suffered unspeakably, their minds, too, became deeply affected by the combined assault of extreme cold and hunger. All human compassion vanished, each thought and cared only for himself and be damned to his comrade. With complete indifference he watched him lie down and die, without emotion he seated himself on his corpse by the fireside.

H.A. Vossler, *With Napoleon in Russia, 1812* (translated by Walter Wallich), London: The Folio Society, 1969, pp. 92–3.

(b) From the 29th Bulletin of the Grande Armée, 3 December 1812

Up to November 6 the weather was perfect and the movement of the army was executed with the greatest success. The cold began on the 7th; from this moment each night we lost several hundred horses who died in bivouac. When we reached Smolensk we had already lost many cavalry and artillery horses. ...

The cold ... worsened suddenly and, on the 14th, 15th and 16th the thermometer showed 16 and 18 degrees below freezing. The roads were covered in ice; horses of the cavalry, artillery and transport perished every night, not in hundreds but in thousands. ... More than 30,000 horses died in a few days; our cavalry found itself on foot; our artillery and transport found themselves without teams. We had to abandon and destroy a good part of our guns, our munitions, and our food supplies.

This army, so fine on the 6th, was very different on the 14th, almost without cavalry, artillery or transportation... We had to march so as not to be forced to a battle which the lack of munitions prevented us from desiring. This difficulty, combined with the excessive cold which suddenly came upon us, made our situation serious. Those men whose temperament was not strong enough to rise above all the twists of fate and fortune, appeared shaken, they lost their gaiety, their good humour, and dreamed only of misfortunes and catastrophes; those made of stronger stuff, preserved their gaiety and their usual outlook and saw a new glory in difficulties to surmount.

The enemy who saw the roads and the traces of this frightful calamity which struck the French army, sought to profit from it. They enveloped all the columns with Cossacks, who, like the Arabs in the desert, robbed the trains and the vehicles that became separated. This contemptible cavalry, which is good at making a noise but which couldn't rout a light infantry company, became formidable only through favourable circumstances. ...

The enemy occupied all the crossings of the Berezina. ... The enemy's general placed his 4 divisions across the different routes where he presumed the French army wished to cross.

At daybreak on the 26th , having deceived the enemy by various movements on the 25th, the Emperor ... had two bridges thrown over the river. The Duke of Reggio [Oudinot] crossed, attacked the enemy and carried on fighting for two hours; the enemy retired. ... General Legrand, a first rate officer, was seriously, but not dangerously wounded. All day during the 26th and 27th the army crossed. ...

Suffice it to say in conclusion that the army needs to re-establish its discipline, to reorganise, to remount its cavalry, artillery and supply trains. Rest is its first need. Supplies and horses arrive. ... The generals, officers and soldiers suffered much from fatigue and hunger. Many lost their baggage as a result of the loss of their horses, others because of ambushes by the Cossacks. The Cossacks have captured many isolated men. ...

In all this activity the Emperor always marched in the midst of his Guard, the cavalry commanded by the marshal Duke of Istria [Bessières], and the infantry commanded by the Duke of Danzig [Lefebvre]. His majesty is satisfied with the good spirit which his Guard showed...

The health of His majesty has never been better.

Le Moniteur, 17 December 1812.

DOCUMENT 17   NAPOLEON'S APPEAL TO HIS 'BROTHER' SOVEREIGNS

This document was issued some two weeks after Napoleon had reinstalled himself as Emperor in Paris. It appears to have been an attempt to forestall war, at least for the moment, and to stress to the monarchs of Europe that he, rather than Louis XVIII, was the choice of the people of France.

Paris, 4 April 1815

Monsieur, my Brother,

You will have learnt, during the course of the last month, of my return to the coasts of France, of my entry into Paris, and of the departure of the Bourbon family. The true nature of these events must now be known Your Majesty. They are the work of an irresistible power, the work of the unanimous will of a great nation conscious of its duties and of its rights. The dynasty that force had reimposed on the French people was no longer suitable for it: the Bourbons did not wish to associate themselves with national feelings or national customs; and France was forced to separate from them. Her voice called for a liberator. The expectation which had decided me to make the greatest of sacrifices was in vain. I returned, and from the spot where I first touched the shore I was carried by the love of my people into the bosom of my capital.

The first need of my heart is to repay so much affection by the maintenance of an honourable peace. The re-establishment of the imperial throne was necessary for the happiness of the French people. My dearest hope is that it may also secure repose for Europe. ... Having provided the world with the spectacle of great contests, it will now please me better to know no other rivalries than those of the advantages of peace, and no other struggle than the crusade for the happiness of peoples. ...

Cor. Nap., XXVIII, no. 21769.

There was little else for Napoleon to do in exile on St Helena but reflect on his past. He did not write a personal memoir, but commented and dictated to a variety of followers and sympathetic listeners. The comte de Las Cases's Mémorial de Saint Hélène *was to become the most celebrated of the publications to result.*

(a) Napoleon on History

20th [November 1816]   'It must be admitted, my dear Las Cases,' said the Emperor to me today, 'it is most difficult to obtain absolute certainties for the purposes of history. Fortunately it is, in general, more a matter of mere curiosity than of real importance. There are so many different kinds of truths! ... The truth of history, so much in request, to which every body eagerly appeals, is to often but a word. At the time of events, during the heat of conflicting passions, it cannot exist; and if, at a later period, all parties are agreed respecting it, it is because those persons who were interested in the events, those who might be able to contradict what is asserted, are no more. What then is, generally speaking, the truth of history? A fable agreed upon. As it has been very ingeniously remarked, there are, in these matters, two essential points, very distinct from each other: the positive facts, and the moral intentions. With respect to the positive facts, it would seem that they ought to be incontrovertible; yet you will not find two accounts agreeing together in relating the same fact: some have remained contested points to this day, and will ever remain so. With regard to moral intentions, how shall we judge them, even admitting the candour of those who relate events? And what will be the case if the narrators be not sincere, or if they should be actuated by interest or passions? I have given an order, but who will be able to read my thoughts, my real intentions? Yet everyone will take up that order, and measure it according to his own scale, or adapt it to his own plans or system. ... And each person will be so certain of what he tells! and the inferior classes of people, who will have received their information from these privileged individuals, will be so certain, in their turn of their correctness! and then the memoirs are digested, memoranda are written, witticisms and anecdotes are circulated; and of such materials is history composed!'

Las Cases, 1823, iv, pp. 251–2.

(b) Napoleon on his intentions

[24th August 1816]   'Peace, concluded at Moscow, would have fulfilled and wound up my hostile expeditions. It would have been, with respect to the grand cause, the term of casualties and the commencement of security. A new horizon, new undertakings, would have unfolded themselves, adapted in every respect, to the well-being and prosperity of all. The foundation of the European system would have been laid, and my only remaining task would have been its organisation.

Satisfied on all these grand points, and everywhere at peace, I should also have had my congress and my holy alliance. These are plans which were stolen from me. In that assembly of all the sovereigns, we should have discussed our interest in a family way, and settled our accounts with the people, as the clerk does with his master.

The cause of the age was victorious, the revolution was accomplished; the only point in question was to reconcile it with what it had not destroyed. But that task belonged to me; I had for a long time been making preparations for it, *at the expense, perhaps, of my popularity.* No matter. I became the arch of the old and new alliance, the natural mediator between the ancient and modern order of things. I maintained the principles and the confidence of the one; I had identified myself with the other. I belonged to both; I should have acted conscientiously in favour of each:

'My glory would have consisted in my equity.'

And, after having enumerated what he would have proposed between sovereign and sovereign, and between sovereigns and their people ... he next took a review of what he would have proposed for the prosperity, the interests, the enjoyments and the well-being of the European confederacy. He wished to establish the same principles, the same system every where. A European code; a court of European appeal, with full powers to redress all wrong decisions, as our's redresses at home those of our tribunals. Money of the same value but with different coins; the same weights, the same measures, the same laws, etc. etc.

'Europe would soon in that manner,' he said, 'have really been but the same people, and every one, who travelled, would have every where found himself in one common country.'...

He concluded: 'On my return to France, in the bosom of my country, at once great, powerful, magnificent, at peace and glorious, I would have proclaimed the immutability of boundaries, all future wars, purely defensive; all new aggrandisement, anti-national. I would have associated my son with the empire; my dictatorship would have terminated, and his constitutional reign commenced. Paris would have been the capital of the world, and the French the envy of nations!'

Las Cases, 1823, iii, pp. 265–7.

(c) Napoleon on his career

[1 May 1816]   '...let them abridge, suppress, and mutilate as much as they please, they will find it very difficult to throw me entirely into the shade. The historian of France cannot pass over the Empire, and, if he have any honesty, he will not fail to render me my share of justice. His task will be easy; the facts speak for themselves: they shine like the sun.

I closed the gulf of anarchy and cleared the chaos. I purified the Revolution, dignified Nations and established Kings. I excited every kind of emulation, rewarded every kind of merit, and extended the limits of glory! This is at least something! And on what point can I be assailed on which an historian could not defend me? Can it be for my intentions? But even here I can find absolution. Can it be for my despotism? It may be demonstrated that Dictatorship was absolutely necessary. Will it be said that I restrained liberty? It can be proved that licentiousness, anarchy, and the greatest irregularities, still haunted the threshold of freedom. Shall I be accused of having been too fond of war? It can be shown that I always received the first attack. Will it be said that I aimed at universal monarchy? It can be proved that this was merely the result of fortuitous circumstances, and that our enemies themselves led me step by step to this determination. Lastly, shall I be blamed for my ambition? This passion I must doubtless be allowed to have possessed, and that in no small degree; but, at the same time, my ambition was of the highest and noblest kind that ever, perhaps, existed! That of establishing and of consecrating the Empire of reason, and the full exercise and complete enjoyment of all the human faculties! And here the historian will probably feel compelled to regret that such ambition should not have been fulfilled and gratified!' Then after a few moments of silent reflection; 'this,' said the Emperor, 'is my whole history in a few words.'

Las Cases, 1823, ii, pp. 196–8.

DOCUMENT 19   REFLECTIONS OF A ROMANTIC

Alfred de Musset (1810–57) was a French Romantic poet, playwright and novelist. The following extract from his La confession d'un enfant du siècle *(1835) contains one of the most striking of the literary reflections on the Napoleonic adventure by a Romantic.*

There was then but one man alive in Europe; all the rest sought to fill their lungs with the air that he had breathed. Each year France made a gift to this man of three hundred thousand young men; it was a tax paid to Caesar, and without this troop behind him, he could not follow his fortune. It was the escort he needed to be able to traverse the world, and then to fall in a little valley on a deserted island beneath a weeping willow.

Never were there so many sleepless nights, as in the time of this man; never have you seen so many desolate mothers leaning over town ramparts; never was there such a silence around those who spoke of death. Yet never was there so much joy, so much life, so many warlike fanfares in every heart. Never were there suns as pure as those that dried all this blood. It is said that God made them for this man, and they are called the suns of Austerlitz. But he made them well enough himself with his ever thundering cannon that left clouds only the day after his battles.

It was the air of this unsullied sky, where so much glory shone, where so much steel gleamed, that the children would breathe. They knew well enough that they were destined for the hecatombs; but they believed Murat invulnerable, and the Emperor had been seen to cross a bridge in a hail of bullets, and it seemed he could not die. And even when you had to die, so what? Death itself was then so beautiful, so magnificent in its smoking crimson! ... All the cradles of France were shields, and so were all the coffins; truly, there were no longer any old men, there were only corpses and demi-gods.

...

Now, seated on a ruined world is a frustrated generation. All these children were drops of a burning blood that has flooded the ground; they were born in the bosom of war, for war. For fifteen years they have dreamed of the snows of Moscow and the sun of the Pyramids. They have never left their towns, but they have been told that through each town gates is the route to a European capital. They had a whole world in their heads; they looked at the ground, the sky, the streets and the roads; everything was empty, and the bells of their parishes rang alone in the distance.

Alfred de Musset, *La confession d'un enfant du siècle* [first published, 1835], Paris: Éditions Garnier Frères, 1962, pp. 2–4.

GLOSSARY

Acte additionnel   Liberal additions made to the imperial constitution during the Hundred Days.

Allgemeines Landrecht   The Prussian General Law Code of 1794. Unlike the Napoleonic Code it did not establish full equality before the law but maintained different provisions for individuals from different social origins.

amalgame   The imperial policies to bring together old enemies from the Revolution and the old regime and also to unite the old nobility with the new created by Napoleon.

auditeurs   The corps of professional officials established for the Council of State in 1803, generally seen as the first rung on the ladder to the leading appointments in the bureaucratic hierarchy.

biens nationaux   'National property', land seized from the Church, from royalty and *émigrés* and/or suspect persons, generally sold on to private buyers (*acquéreurs*).

Chouan   Royalist insurgents, mainly in the west of France and especially Brittany.

Chouannerie   Royalist uprising in the west.

contrabande   Smuggling, smuggled goods.

contribution foncière   Land tax.

contribution personnelle mobilière   Property tax.

décadi   The tenth day of the *decade* and the weekly rest day, as designated in the ten-day week of the Revolutionary Calendar.

donataire   Recipient of a *dotation*.

dotation   Territory seized by Napoleon in his conquered territories and distributed to a loyal follower, its revenues to be passed on through the male line of recipient's family.

droits réunis   Indirect taxes on commodities such as alcoholic drinks, salt, tobacco.

émigrés   Individuals who left France during the Revolution, not necessarily nobles.

État civil   The registry for the registration of births, marriages and deaths that became a state monopoly during the Revolution.

fédérés   Individuals who came together, largely spontaneously, during the Hundred Days to defend the empire. They were numerous in some workers' districts, notably in Paris, and contributed significantly to the idea of 'popular Bonapartism' among workers.

fraude   Trafficking in permitted goods, but without paying the required duties or completing the required paper work.

garnisaire The quartering of troops on families or villages, at the latter's expense, generally as a punishment for draft evasion.

Grand Army (*la Grande Armée*) First used in 1805 it refers technically only to a mass army commanded by Napoleon in person, but is often used as a synonym for the entire imperial army.

Lettre de cachet Sealed administrative letter, signed by the monarch and counter-signed by a minister, which authorised the detention of an individual without recourse to the courts.

Lieutenant-général de police de Paris The magistrate charged with the supervision of the police of Paris under the old regime.

livret (livret ouvrier) A worker's pass book, issued by the police or a municipality. It had to be handed to an employer when a person began to work for him, and signed when the person left his employ. No person could be hired without a *livret* signed by the previous employer. A worker without a *livret* was considered a vagabond and was liable to six months' imprisonment.

octroi Duties levied on consumer goods entering the main towns and cities of France.

pays conquis Territories conquered by France and made subject states of the Empire.

pays réunis Non-French territories annexed to, and fully incorporated as parts of France.

ralliement The rallying and winning over of individuals (*ralliés*) to Bonaparte either at the time of *Brumaire* or later.

Reichsdeputationshauptschluss The main resolution of the *Reichsdeputation*, the committee of eight appointed at the suggestion of Francis II, the Holy Roman Emperor, to negotiate compensation for the German princes dispossessed by the French occupation of the left bank of the Rhine. The resolution significantly reorganised west and south Germany.

Senatus consultum (pl. consulta) A procedure that empowered the Senate, through its right to preserve and amend the constitution, to sanction constitutional change and new laws. It was used increasingly to bypass other legislative bodies.

WHO'S WHO

Alexander I (1777–1825) Tsar of Russia. Educated at the court of his grandmother, Catherine the Great, where he absorbed much Enlightenment thought. Succeeded to the throne on his father's assassination in 1801. His programme of administrative, educational and social reform achieved little. In foreign affairs he reversed his father's policies and joined alliances against France. He was greatly impressed by Napoleon when they met at Tilsit, but strains rapidly developed in his new alliance with France. He played a key role in the final coalitions against Napoleon and in the Congress of Vienna. Inspired by a fanatical pietism he proposed the Holy Alliance bonding European monarchs together. The last years of his reign saw the eclipse of his early enlightened ideas.

Barras, Paul (1755–1829) French politician. Born into the nobility and served in the old regime army. Sided with the Revolution and became a deputy in 1792. Involved with brutal repression of counter revolution in Marseilles and with recapture of Toulon. A key figure in the coup that toppled Robespierre, he played a major political role during the Thermidorian period and served as a Director. Napoleon forced him out of politics and, in 1810, into exile. He was noted for his disreputable lifestyle and for corruption.

Beauharnais, Eugène de (1781–1824) Son of Josephine, stepson of Napoleon. Initially resentful of his mother's marriage to General Bonaparte, he served as an aide-de-camp in the Italian campaign (1796–97). Created a prince on the formation of the Empire (1804) and Viceroy of Italy (1805) he proved to be an able administrator and a courageous and competent soldier. He commanded Italian troops during the Russian campaign. On Napoleon's first abdication he retired to Munich. He took no part in the Hundred Days.

Beauharnais, Hortense Eugénie de (1783–1837) Daughter of Josephine, step-daughter of Napoleon. Married Louis Bonaparte (1802), and bore him three sons, the youngest of whom, Charles Louis Napoleon (1808–1873) was to become the Emperor Napoleon III.

Bernadotte, Jean-Baptiste-Jules (1763–1844) French soldier, subsequently Charles XIV, King of Sweden and Norway. The son of a Gascon avocat he enlisted in the army in 1780 reaching non-commissioned rank before the Revolution. Served in Revolutionary wars reaching the rank of general. Married Joseph Bonaparte's sister-in-law (1798), remained aloof during *Brumaire*, and not always in favour with Napoleon. Marshal and governor of Hanover (1804), Prince of Ponte Corvo (1806). Elected Crown Prince of Sweden to replace the childless Charles XIII (1810) and, during the latter's illness acted as regent. Led Swedish troops against Napoleon in 1813 and negotiated with Britain, Prussia and Russia for the Swedish acquisition of Norway. Appears to have hoped he might replace Napoleon in France in 1814. Succeeded to Swedish throne in 1818.

Blücher, Gebhard Leberecht, Prince von (1742–1819) Prussian soldier. Born in Rostock he joined the Swedish army aged 14, entering Prussian service when captured by them in 1760. An outspoken and courageous cavalry commander he fought in the Revolutionary wars and in the disastrous campaign of 1806. In trouble for his verbal attacks on France in the years following the Prussian defeat, he went on to command Prussian troops in the campaign of 1813–14 and at Waterloo.

Bonaparte, Caroline (1782–1839) Youngest sister of Napoleon. Married Murat (1800). During his absences she ruled autocratically first the Grand Duchy of Berg and then the Kingdom of Naples. Showed herself greedy for honours. With the death of Murat she took the title Countess of Lipona (an anagram of Napoli).

Bonaparte, Elisa (1777–1820) Eldest sister of Napoleon. Married the Corsican Felix Bacciochi (1797). Greedy for honours the couple received the small principality of Piombino (1805) then Tuscany (1809). She proved an enthusiastic reformer of her territories, Bacciochi had little say. She offered to join Napoleon on St Helena, but finally settled in Trieste as the Countess of Compignano.

Bonaparte, Jerome (1784–1860) Youngest brother of Napoleon. Had first marriage, to an American, annulled by Napoleon who did not approve, then married daughter of King of Württemberg. Created King of Westphalia (1807). Held junior command in the Russian campaign. Rallied to Napoleon during the Hundred Days and fought at Waterloo. Forcibly separated from his wife following the defeat he spent the next 30 years travelling and then settling in Trieste. Returned to France in 1847.

Bonaparte, Joseph (1768–1844) Eldest brother of Napoleon. Began diplomatic career under Directory. Created King of Naples (1806), then King of Spain (1808). Sought to protect his subjects from some of the more severe of his brother's exactions. Forced from Spain by Wellington; became Lieutenant-General of France in 1814. Retired from public life on the first restoration.

Bonaparte, Louis (1778–1846) Brother of Napoleon. Served as an aide to his brother in the Italian and Egyptian campaigns. General (1804), Governor of Paris (1805), King of Holland (1806). Had serious differences with Napoleon when he sought to pursue independent policies and then when his marriage to Hortense de Beauharnais broke down. Abdicated in 1810. Spent most of remainder of his life in Rome following literary pursuits.

Bonaparte, Lucien (1775–1840) Brother of Napoleon. Played key role in coup of *Brumaire*, but more liberal than Napoleon and largely retired from public life during the Consulate. Napoleon thought his wife lacked the appropriate pedigree, but he was given title of Prince of Canino and lived in Papal territories until their annexation. Taking ship for the USA he was captured by the British. Rallied to Napoleon during the Hundred Days. Spent most of the remainder of his life in Italy.

Bonaparte, Maria Letizia (c. 1750–1836) Mother of Napoleon. Born Maria Letizia Ramolino into Corsican family of Florentine origin. Married Carlo Buonaparte (1764) by whom she had 12 children (4 dying in infancy). Named *Madame mère* (March 1805), the title reserved for dowager queens during the old regime. Joined Napoleon on Elba (1814) and followed him to Paris during the Hundred Days. Retired to Rome living under Papal protection.

Bonaparte, Pauline (1780–1825)   Sister of Napoleon. Noted for her beauty and her succession of lovers. Married General Leclerc (1797) and travelled on campaign with him. Leclerc died in 1801 and she married the Italian nobleman, Prince Borghese, in 1803. The couple were given the principality of Guastalla in 1806. After Waterloo she joined her mother in Rome. She was intending to travel to St Helena when news of her brother's death arrived.

Cadoudal, Georges (1771–1804)   Chouan leader. Involved in the Vendéan insurrection against the Revolution in 1793, he subsequently organised the Chouan guerrillas in Brittany. The First Consul tried to win his allegiance with a general's commission and a pension, but Cadoudal continued to conspire for the restoration of the Bourbons. He was captured in Paris in March 1804 and executed.

Cambacérès, Jean-Jacques Règis de (1753–1824)   French politician. Born into the nobility in Montpellier he studied law. Elected to the National Convention in 1792 he subsequently held posts during the Thermidorian regime and the Directory. Consul (1799), Arch Chancellor of the Empire (1804), duc de Parma (1808). He was able and intelligent. He was particularly interested in, and involved with, legal reform. He also made a lot of money. Supervised the imperial administration during Napoleon's absence, and was prepared to speak his mind, advising against the invasions of both Spain and Russia. Served reluctantly during the Hundred Days, and was exiled under the second restoration. In 1818 he had his French citizenship restored and returned to France where he spent the rest of his life in a very wealthy retirement.

Castlereagh, Robert Stewart, Viscount (1769–1822)   British politician. The son of an Ulster landowner he held a variety of government posts first in Ireland and then in the British government. British Foreign Secretary from 1812, he played a key role in organising the final coalitions against Napoleon and represented Britain at the Congress of Vienna.

Charles (Carlos) IV (1748–1819)   King of Spain. Succeeded to the throne in 1768 in place of his insane elder brother. Tended to leave the tasks of ruling to his wife, Maria Luisa of Parma, and the royal favourite Manuel de Godoy. Generally supported Napoleon 1801–08. Forced to abdicate by his son, Ferdinand, in 1808, he hoped Napoleon would reinstate him. Instead Napoleon deposed the family and put Joseph Bonaparte on the throne. Eventually retired to Rome, where he died.

Chateaubriand, François-René, vicomte de (1768–1848)   French politician and man of letters. Born into a noble family in St. Malo, he was initially sympathetic to the Revolution. Visited America, returning to join the émigré army in 1791, he was wounded in 1793. In England (1793–1800), returned as a *rallié* in 1800. Published *Le Génie du Christianisme* (1802). Resigned from diplomatic post following the execution of d'Enghien. Exiled from Paris (1807) for an article critical of Napoleon. Resumed public and political life during the Restoration serving in several ministerial and ambassadorial posts. *Mémoires d'outre-tombe* (Memoirs from beyond the Grave) is his best remembered work with considerable critical comment on Napoleon. It began to be published shortly after his death.

Constant (de Rebecque), Henri Benjamin (1767–1830)   French man of letters and liberal politician. A key figure in the liberal republican circles that influenced the Directory. Together with his lover, Madame de Staël, he became a critic of the First Consul going into exile in 1803 and spending the next ten years mainly in Germany. He returned to France during the first restoration and stayed during the Hundred Days when he drafted the *Acte additionelle*. Served as a liberal deputy throughout the restoration and briefly held office following the Revolution of 1830.

Dalberg, Karl Theodor von (1744–1817)   German Catholic cleric. Before the Revolution he was a leader of the Catholic Enlightenment. Archbishop-Elector of Mainz (1802) he was the only ecclesiastical prince to survive the secularisation of 1803. He tried initially to revive the administration of the Holy Roman Empire to provide a central government for Germany, but then sided with Napoleon. Prince-Primate of the Confederation of the Rhine (1806) and Grand Duke of Frankfurt (1810). He tried to turn the *Rheinbund* into a federation, but found the princes were not prepared to give up their independence. After the battle of Leipzig he went into exile in Zurich.

David, Jacques-Louis (1748–1825)   French artist. Before the Revolution he was noted for his large canvases depicting classical subjects. Prominent during Revolution as a deputy in the National Convention, the artistic chronicler of revolutionary events and the organiser of the great republican festivals. Began long association with General Bonaparte in 1797. Appointed First Painter to the Emperor (1804). Forced into exile in the second restoration he settled in Brussels and returned to painting classical subjects.

Enghien, Louis Antoine Henri de Bourbon-Condé, duc d' (1772–1804)   French nobleman (see above, p. 81).

Ferdinand (Fernando) VII (1784–1833)   King of Spain. Eldest son of Charles IV he developed an intense dislike of his parents and their favourite, Godoy. Arrested for involvement in a conspiracy in 1807, he turned the tables on his parents and forced his father to abdicate in 1808. But then he was forced to renounce throne by Napoleon (1808), living in luxurious exile in France until his restoration (1814). On his return he alienated liberals and loyal army officers. A series of attempted coups reached a climax in 1820 when he was compelled to accept the liberal constitution. He was restored to full power by French intervention, but then alienated the French by pursuing a ferocious vengeance.

Fouché, Joseph (1759–1820)   French politician and minister of police. Born Nantes, the son of a merchant sea captain he was educated by the Oratorians and became one of their lay teachers. A deputy in the national Convention in 1792 he was prominent in suppressing counter-revolution and in the dechristianising campaign. Involved in the overthrow of Robespierre, he disappeared into obscurity for a couple of years. He re-emerged as a diplomat and police administrator under the Directory. Minister of Police (1799–1802 and 1804–10). Duc d'Otranto (1809). In 1810 he was dismissed from the Police ministry for secret communication with Britain and was banished to Aix. Governor of the Illyrian provinces (1813). Returned to Paris during the first restoration, Minister of Police again during the Hundred Days, but helped to re-establish the monarchy again in 1815. Banished in 1816 he retired to Trieste.

Francis (Franz) II (Holy Roman Emperor until 1806) *Francis I* (of Austria from 1804) *(1768–1835)* Succeeded as Holy Roman Emperor in 1792 and participated in all of the coalitions against Revolutionary France. Took the title of hereditary Emperor of Austria in 1804, and this made it easier to give up the title of Holy Roman Emperor when events compelled this in 1806. Not a brilliant ruler or administrator, but hard-working and patient. From 1809 he relied heavily on Metternich for foreign affairs and gave him considerable leeway. After Napoleon's defeat he became closely associated with reactionary policies across Europe.

Frederick William (Friedrich Wilhelm) III (1770–1840) King of Prussia. As a soldier, participated in the early campaigns against Revolutionary France. Succeeded to the throne in 1797. Not a particularly strong or able man, he received considerable strength from his wife, Louise, the daughter of the Prince of Mecklenburg-Strelitz. She helped him through the disaster of 1806 and encouraged him to appoint reformers like Stein and Scharnhorst. She died in 1810. During the German War of Liberation he promised his people a constitution, but never kept the promise. Following Napoleon's defeat he followed the reactionary lead of Prussia and Austria.

Gros, Antoine-Jean (1771–1835) French artist, responsible for some of the most dramatic paintings representing incidents in Napoleon's career. The son of a painter of miniatures he entered David's studio as a student in 1785. Travelled with Napoleon's army on many occasions from 1796. His fortunes declined with the fall of the Empire and the decline in interest in neo-classical art.

Josephine, French Empress (1763–1814) Born Marie-Rose Josephine Tascher de la Pagerie into the lesser nobility of Martinique. Married vicomte de Beauharnais (1779) by whom she had two children (Eugène and Hortense). Arrested during the Terror, when her husband was guillotined. Married General Bonaparte (1796). Noted for her generosity and lack of malice she was often subjected to petty jealousy by some of the Bonapartes. Divorced by Napoleon for dynastic reasons (1809) she nevertheless retained the title of empress and an annual income of 80,000 francs. She retired to Malmaison, where she died.

Jourdan, Jean-Baptiste (1762–1833) French soldier, son of a surgeon. General in Revolutionary armies. Member of the Council of 500 (1797). Framed the conscription law of 1798 (*la loi Jourdan*). Appointed Marshal 1804, becoming a close adviser to Joseph Bonaparte in Naples and then in Spain. Refused to serve on the court-martial of Marshal Ney following the second restoration. Created count and member of the Chamber of Peers (1819). Welcomed the Revolution of 1830.

Las Cases, Emmanuel Auguste Dieudonné, comte de (1766–1842) Napoleon's best-known memorialist. Born into the minor nobility he served briefly in the navy of the old regime and, during the Revolution, he was in the *émigré* army. He returned to France during the Consulate. Appointed Chamberlain to Napoleon (1809) and count (1810). He rallied to the Emperor in the Hundred Days, and then travelled with him to St Helena. In 1816 he was arrested and removed from the island for criticism of the governor. Returned to France on Napoleon's death, elected to the Chamber of Deputies in 1831.

Lebrun, Charles-François (1739–1824) French politician. Educated in law he was involved with attempts to reform the old regime monarchy in the 1770s. A moderate reformer during the Revolution he was imprisoned during the Terror and served in the Council of Ancients during the Directory. Consul, then Arch Treasurer of the Empire (1804). Governor-general of Liguria (1805–06) organising its annexation to France. Disapproved of the imperial nobility, but was persuaded to accept title duc de Piacenza. Governor-general of Holland following its annexation (1810). Rallied to Napoleon during the Hundred Days. Reinstated to the Chamber of Peers in 1819.

Louis XVIII (1755–1824) King of France. Brother of Louis XVI. Critical of the way the Revolution was developing and went into exile in 1791. Technically succeeded his nephew, Louis XVII, when he disappeared in 1795. Returned to France as king following the fall of Napoleon. During the restoration he attempted to steer a middle course between the reactionary faction around his younger brother (the comte d'Artois, later Charles X) and more liberal elements.

Malet, Claude-François de (1754–1812) French soldier and conspirator against Napoleon (see above, pp. 22 and 108).

Marie Louise (1791–1847) Austrian princess and French empress. Daughter of Francis I of Austria. Married Napoleon (1810) and bore him a son (1811). Following Napoleon's first abdication she travelled to Vienna with her son, and remained there during the Hundred Days. Granted the Italian duchies of Parma, Piacenza and Guastalla (1818) which she ruled in an enlightened fashion with the Austrian general Adam Neipperg whom she married on Napoleon's death, bearing him four children. On Neipperg's death she married the comte de Bombelles.

Metternich, Clemens Lothar Wenzel, Prince (1773–1859) Austrian politician. Brought up in the Rhineland where his father served as the Habsburg representative to several principalities. Made a good marriage in Vienna (1795) and embarked on a diplomatic career. Ambassador to Berlin (1803), to Paris (1806). Appointed Minister of State in Vienna (August 1809) and Foreign Minister (October 1809). Became a key diplomatic figure in Europe for the next 40 years, always cautiously preserving a balance of power and wary of a single power become too strong and dominant. Created hereditary prince (1813). A central figure at the Congress of Vienna.

Moncey, Bon-Adrien (1754–1842) French soldier. Son of an *avocat* in the *Parlement* of Besançon he gave up the study of law for a military career in 1769. Still a junior officer at the outbreak of the Revolution, he was made general in 1793. Inspector General of the Gendarmerie (1801); marshal (1804); duc de Conegliano (1808). As commander of the Gendarmerie he clashed regularly with Fouché over authority in policing matters. Did not participate in the Hundred Days, but was deprived of his marshalate for refusing to serve on Ney's court martial. Subsequently (1816) reinstated and commanded a corps in the Spanish campaign of 1823.

Murat, Joachim (1767–1815) French soldier, King of Naples. Son of a Gascon innkeeper; rejected the study of canon law for the army. A flamboyant cavalry commander he served alongside Napoleon from *Vendémiaire*. Married Caroline

Bonaparte (1800). Created marshal (1804). Grand Duke of Berg and Cleves (1806). King of Naples (1808). Relations grew frosty with Napoleon but he served in the Russian campaign then, following the battle of Leipzig, he sought separate negotiations with the allies. Diplomatic discussions continued until the Hundred Days when he tried to secure his throne by mobilising the Neapolitan army and calling for a united Italy. He was defeated by the Austrians, escaped to France where Napoleon refused his services. Metternich offered him a position and a pension. He rejected it, returned to southern Italy with a small force in October 1815, was captured, court-martialled and shot.

Ney, Michel (1769–1815)   French soldier. Son of a cooper, began life as a clerk, enlisted in army in 1788. Rose to rank of general during the Revolution. Marshal (1804), duc d'Elchingen (1808). Noted for his impetuosity and bravery – Napoleon called him 'the bravest of the brave'. Created Prince of Moscow on the evening of the battle of Borodino. Commanded the rearguard during the retreat from Moscow. Played a key role in persuading Napoleon to abdicate in 1814 and served Louis XVIII. Promised to arrest Napoleon on his return from Elba, but defected. Fought at Waterloo, after which royalists insisted that he be court-martialled. He was sentenced and shot.

Paoli, Pasquale (1726–1807)   Corsican patriot. Was virtual ruler of Corsica 1757–68 having driven Genoese out of all but a few coastal towns. Sought to prevent French annexation in 1768 but was forced to seek refuge in Britain until the Revolution. Invited to return by the revolutionaries he was appointed governor of Corsica. But the island was torn by faction. He was denounced to the Convention. Civil war followed. He reluctantly received British assistance, but eventually went into exile in London. He was a hero to the young Napoleon.

Pius VII (Luigi Barnabà Chiaramonti) (1740–1823)   Pope. Entered Benedictine order in 1758, Bishop of Tivoli (1782), Bishop of Imola and cardinal (1785), Pope (1800). Relatively liberal and hoped to restore links with France by the Concordat. Hoped to get the Organic Articles amended by agreeing to officiate at Napoleon's coronation. Thereafter relations with Napoleon deteriorated. Excommunicated Napoleon when Rome was occupied and annexed, and was arrested and imprisoned by the French. Enacted some liberal reforms when restored on Napoleon's fall, but his policies were mainly critical of French and Enlightenment ideas.

Savary, Anne-Jean-Marie-René (1774–1833)   French soldier and police minister. Son of a cavalry officer he volunteered for the army in 1790. Aide-de-camp to Napoleon after the battle of Marengo. General (1803), duc de Rovigo (1808), Minister of Police (1810). He was used by Napoleon to carry out a variety of unpleasant tasks (e.g. the court-martial and execution of d'Enghien). Captured by the conspirators during the Malet plot, but Napoleon continued to rely on him and his unswerving loyalty. Returned to military life after the 1830 Revolution serving briefly as commander-in-chief in Algeria (1831).

Sieyès, Emmanuel-Joseph (1748–1836)   French politician. Entered the Church rising to be vicar general and chancellor of the diocese of Chartres. Well known for his liberal opinions. Published the important pamphlet *Qu'est-ce que le tiers état? (What is the Third Estate?)* on the eve of the Revolution and contributed to the Declaration of the Rights of Man and Citizen. Elected a deputy in 1789 and 1792. Member of the Council of 500. A Director (1799). One of the *Brumaire* conspirators and one of the first members of the Consulate. Became a senator, but spent many of the Empire years in retirement. Left France on the restoration of the Bourbons, returning after the Revolution of 1830.

De Staël (or de Staël-Holstein), Germaine (1766–1817) French novelist and critic of Napoleon. Daughter of Jacques Necker, Genevan banker and finance minister of Louis XVI. Published her first novel in 1786. The same year she married a Swedish diplomat, later ambassador to France, Baron de Staël-Holstein. Sympathetic to liberal ideas of Revolution, left France during the Terror, returned on fall of Robespierre. Opened a celebrated salon in rue de Bac in Paris during the Directory, and began an affair with Benjamin Constant. Widowed in 1802. Initially sympathetic to General Bonaparte, she increasingly became a critic during the Consulate. Banned from the vicinity of Paris (1803) she spent the next decade either travelling or in the family home at Coppet (Switzerland). She married a Swiss officer 23 years her junior (1811). Returned to Paris on the restoration and reopened her salon (1816).

Stein, Heinrich Friedrich Karl, Baron vom und zum (1757–1831) German politican. Entered Prussian service in 1780. Criticised Frederick William following 1806 disaster and was dismissed. Reinstated after Tilsit as Minister of Home affairs with wide powers. Launched a major reform programme freeing serfs, abolishing caste distinctions, reorganising land tenure and municipal government. Encouraged military reforms. Napoleon put pressure on for his dismissal. Fled to Austria (January 1809) then to Russia. Led administration of Prussia after French withdrawal. Retired after Congress of Vienna.

Talleyrand (or Talleyrand-Périgord), Charles-Maurice (1754–1838) French politican. Born into French nobility. A club foot ruled out a military career so he entered the Church. Bishop of Autun (1788) and prominent among the liberal clergy in the early years of the Revolution. Renounced bishopric for a diplomatic career (1792). Foreign minister for the Directory (1797–99) then under Napoleon (1799–1807). Noted for his corruption and cynicism but worked to get laws relaxed against *émigrés*, royalists and non-juring clergy. Also sought to moderate Napoleon's foreign policies and his treatment of defeated enemies. Retired in 1807, but negotiated the return of Louis XVIII and represented France at the Congress of Vienna. Briefly served as Foreign Minister during the second restoration, then as High Chamberlain. After the Revolution of 1830 he became ambassador in London.

Wellington, Arthur Wellesley, 1st Duke of (1769–1852) British soldier. Born in Ireland, fourth son of the Earl of Mornington. Joined the army as an ensign (1787), lieutenant-colonel (by purchase, 1793). Fought in the Low Countries (1794–95) then in India where he gained note and distinction. A junior, but successful, commander of the first expedition to Portugal (1808), he returned the following year. Fought a series of successful campaigns against a succession of French generals in Portugal and Spain. Commanded allied armies in Belgium in 1815. Military success brought him wealth and honours, count (1809), earl (1812), duke (1814), prince (of the Netherlands, 1815). Subsequently pursued a political career; prime minister (1828).

Yorck von Wartenburg, Hans David Ludwig (1759–1830)   German soldier of English extraction. Joined the Prussian army in 1772, dismissed for insubordination (1779), served in Dutch army until allowed to rejoin Prussian (1785). Wounded during the campaign of 1806. Commanded one of the Prussian corps assigned to assist in the Russian campaign, signed the Convention of Tauroggen with the Russians (30 December 1812) which made his men neutral. Given the title von Wartenburg following his service in the German War of Liberation, then created a count (1814) and field marshal (1821).

THE REVOLUTIONARY CALENDAR

The Revolutionary Calendar technically began Year I of the Republic on 22 September 1792, the day following the abolition of the monarchy. The calendar consisted of 12 months each of 30 days, subdivided into 3 weeks each of ten days (*décadi*). An additional five days were included at the end of each year to make up 365 days, but there was no allowance for leap-years making precise concordance difficult from the mid-1790s. Each month was named after a significant element of the season in which it fell, thus:

Vendémiaire	September–October	Vintage
Brumaire	October–November	Fog
Frimaire	November–December	Frost
Nivôse	December–January	Snow
Pluviôse	January–February	Rain
Ventôse	February–March	Wind
Germinal	March–April	Germination
Floréal	April–May	Flowers
Prairial	May–June	Meadows
Messidor	June–July	Harvest
Thermidor	July–August	Heat
Fructidor	August–September	Fruit

BIBLIOGRAPHY

(This bibliography concentrates on English-language works. Wide-ranging, readily available, recent volumes that are particularly useful for students are indicated with an asterisk thus *.)

Primary Sources and Collections

Arnold, Eric A. Jr (ed.) (1994) *A Documentary Survey of Napoleonic France*. Lanham, MD: University Press of America.

Dwyer, Philip G. and McPhee, Peter (eds) (2002) *The French Revolution and Napoleon: A Source Book*. London: Routledge.

Herold, J. Christopher (ed.) (1955) *The Mind of Napoleon: A Selection from his Written and Spoken Words*. New York and London: Columbia University Press.

Dieudonné, Emmanuel Auguste, comte de Las Cases (1823) *Mémorial de Sainte Hélène: Journal of the Private Life and Conversations of the Emperor Napoleon at Saint Helena*, 4 vols. London: Henry Colburn & Co.

Thompson, J.M. (ed.) (1998) *Napoleon's Letters*, London: Prion Books (first published as *Napoleon Self-Revealed*, 1934).

Secondary Texts: Books and Articles

Alexander, R.S. (1991) *Bonapartism and the Revolutionary Tradition in France: The Fédérés of 1815*. Cambridge: Cambridge University Press.

Alexander, R.S. (2001) *Napoleon*. London: Arnold.

Arnold, Eric A. Jr (1979) *Fouché. Napoleon and the General Police*. Washington, DC: University Press of America.

*Bergeron, Louis (1981) *France under Napoleon* (translated by R.R. Palmer). Princeton, NJ: Princeton University Press.

*Broers, Michael (1996) *Europe under Napoleon 1799–1815*. London: Arnold.

Broers, Michael (1997) *Napoleonic Imperialism and the Savoyard Monarchy 1773–1821: State Building in Piedmont*. Lewiston, NY: Edwin Mellen Press.

Broers, Michael (2001a) Napoleon, Charlemagne, and Lotharingia: Acculturation and the Boundaries of Napoleonic Europe. *Historical Journal*, 44: 135–54.

Broers, Michael (2001b) Cultural Imperialism in a European Context? Political Culture and Cultural Politics in Napoleonic Italy. *Past and Present*, 170: 152–80.

Broers, Michael (2002) *The Politics of Religion in Italy: The war against God. 1801–1814*. London: Routledge.

Butel, Paul (1991) Revolution and the urban economy: maritime cities and continental cities. In Alan Forrest and Peter Jones (eds), *Reshaping France: Town, Country and Region during the French Revolution*. Manchester: Manchester University Press.

Carrington, Dorothy (1986) *Napoleon and his Parents: On the Threshold of History*. London: Viking.

Chandler, David G. (1966) *The Campaigns of Napoleon*. London: Weidenfeld & Nicolson.

Cobb, Richard (1970) *The Police and the People: French Popular Protest 1789–1815*. Oxford: Oxford University Press.

Cole, Laurence (2000) Nation, Anti-Enlightenment, and Religious Revival in Austria: Tyrol in the 1790s. *Historical Journal*, 43: 475–97

Collins, Irene (1979) *Napoleon and his Parliaments 1800–1815*. London: Edward Arnold.

Connelly, Owen (1965) *Napoleon's Satellite Kingdoms*. New York: The Free Press.

Connelly, Owen (1988) *Blundering to Glory: Napoleon's Military Campaigns*. Wilmington, Del.: SR Books (revised edn, 1999).

Crook, Malcolm (2003) Confidence from below? Collaboration and resistance in the Napoleonic plebiscites. In Rowe (2003).

Crouzet, François (1964) Wars, blockade and economic change in Europe, 1792–1815. *Journal of Economic History*, 24: 567–88.

Daly, Gavin (2001) *Inside Napoleonic France: State and Society in Rouen, 1800–1815*. Aldershot: Ashgate.

Dunne, John (2000) Napoleon's 'mayoral problem': Aspects of state-community relations in post-revolutionary France. *Modern and Contemporary French History*, 8: 479–91.

*Dwyer, Philip G. (ed.) (2001) *Napoleon and Europe*. London: Longman.

Dwyer, Philip G. (2002) From Corsican nationalist to French Revolutionary: Problems of identity in the writings of the young Napoleon, 1785–1793. *French History*, 16: 132–52.

Ellis, Geoffrey (1981) *Napoleon's Continental Blockade: The Case of Alsace*. Oxford: Clarendon Press.

Ellis, Geoffrey (1983) Rhine and Loire: Napoleonic elites and social order. In Gwynne Lewis and Colin Lucas (eds), *Beyond the Terror: Essays in French Regional and Social History*. Cambridge: Cambridge University Press.

*Ellis, Geoffrey (1997) *Napoleon*. London: Longman.

*Ellis, Geoffrey (2003) *The Napoleonic Empire* (2nd edn). London: Palgrave.

Emsley, Clive(1987) Policing the streets of early nineteenth-century Paris. *French History*, 1: 257–82.

Emsley, Clive (1999) *Gendarmes and the State in Nineteenth-Century Europe*. Oxford: Oxford University Press.

Esdaile, Charles J. (1995) *The Wars of Napoleon*. London: Longman.

Esdaile, Charles J. (2004) *Fighting Napoleon: Guerrillas, Bandits and Adventurers in Spain, 1808–1814*, London: Yale University Press.

Eyck, F.G. (1986) *Loyal Rebels: Andreas Hofer and the Tyrolean Uprising of 1809*. Lanham, Md.: University Press of America.

Finley, Milton (1994) *The Most Monstrous of Wars: Napoleonic Guerrilla War in Southern Italy 1806–1811*. Columbia, SC: University of South Carolina Press.

Forrest, Alan (1989) *Conscripts and Deserters: The Army and French Society during the Revolution and Empire*. Oxford: Oxford University Press.

Forrest, Alan (2002) *Napoleon's Men: The Soldiers of the Revolution and Empire*. London: Hambledon & London.

Gates, David (1997) *The Napoleonic Wars 1803–1815*. London: Arnold.

Geyl, Pieter (1949) *Napoleon: For and Against*. London: Jonathan Cape.

Grab, Alexander (1995a) State power, brigandage and rural resistance in Napoleonic Italy. *European History Quarterly*, 25: 39–70.

Grab, Alexander (1995b) Army, state and society: Conscription and desertion in Napoleonic Italy (1802–1814). *Journal of Modern History*, 67: 25–54.

*Grab, Alexander (2003) *Napoleon and the Transformation of Europe*. London: Palgrave.

Holtman, Robert B. (1967) *The Napoleonic Revolution*. Philadelphia, PA: J.B. Lippincott.

Jourdan, Annie (1996) Napoleon and History. *French History*, 10: 334–54.

Jourdan, Annie (1998) *Napoléon: héros, imperator, mécène*. Paris: Aubier.

Jourdan, Annie (2000) Images de Napoléon: un *imperator* en quête de légitimité. *Modern and Contemporary France*, 8: 433–44

Laven, David and Riall, Lucy (eds) (2000) *Napoleon's Legacy: Problems of Government in Restoration Europe*. Oxford and New York: Berg.

Lefebvre, Georges (1969) *Napoleon* (translated H.F. Stockhold), 2 vols. London: Routledge & Kegan Paul.

Le Goff, T.J.A. and Sutherland, D.M.G. (1991) The Revolution and the rural economy. In Alan Forrest and Peter Jones (eds), *Reshaping France: Town, Country and Region during the French Revolution*. Manchester: Manchester University Press.

*Lyons, Martyn (1994) *Napoleon Bonaparte and the Legacy of the French Revolution*. London: Macmillan.

McLynn, Frank (1997) *Napoleon: A Biography*. London: Jonathan Cape.

Nipperdey, Thomas (1996) *Germany from Napoleon to Bismarck 1800–1866* (translated by Daniel Nolan). Dublin: Gill & Macmillan.

Parker, Harold T. (1971) The formation of Napoleon's personality: An exploratory essay. *French Historical Studies*, 7: 6–26.

Parker, Harold T. (2001) Napoleon's youth and rise to power. In Dwyer (2001).

Prendergast, Christopher (1997) *Napoleon and History Painting: Antoine-Jean Gros's 'La bataille d'Eylau'*. Oxford: Clarendon Press.

Richardson, Frank (1972) *Napoleon: Bisexual Emperor*. London: William Kimber.

Rowe, Michael (1999) Between Empire and home town: Napoleonic rule on the Rhine 1799–1814. *Historical Journal*, 42: 643–74.

Rowe, Michael (ed.) (2003) *Collaboration and Resistance in Napoleonic Europe: State Formation in an Age of Upheaval, c.1800–1815*. London: Palgrave.

Schroeder, Paul W. (1994) *The Transformation of European Politics 1763–1848*. Oxford: Clarendon Press.

Sibalis, Michael (2001) The Napoleonic Police State. In Dwyer (2001).

Tulard, Jean (1984) *Napoleon: The Myth of the Saviour* (translated by Teresa Waugh). London: Weidenfeld & Nicolson.

Whitcomb, Edward A. (1974) Napoleon's Prefects. *American Historical Review*, 79: 1089–1118.

Whitcomb, Edward A. (1979) *Napoleon's Diplomatic Service*. Durham, NC: Duke University Press.

Wilson-Smith, Timothy (1996) *Napoleon and his Artists*. London: Constable.

Woloch, Isser (1986) Napoleonic conscription: State power and civil society. *Past and Present*, 111: 101–29.

*Woloch, Isser (1994) *The New Regime: Transformations of the French Civic Culture, 1789–1820s*. New York: Norton.

*Woloch, Isser (2001a) *Napoleon and his Collaborators*. New York: Norton.

Woloch, Isser (2001b) The Napoleonic regime and French society. In Dwyer (2001).

Woolf, Stuart (1989) French civilization and ethnicity in the Napoleonic Empire. *Past and Present*, 124: 96–120.

* Woolf, Stuart (1991) *Napoleon's Integration of Europe*. London: Routledge.

Woolf, Stuart (1992) The construction of a European world-view in the Revolutionary-Napoleonic period. *Past and Present*, 137: 72–101.

INDEX

SEMINAR STUDIES IN HISTORY

General Editors: Clive Emsley & Gordon Martel

The series was founded by Patrick Richardson in 1966. Between 1980 and 1996 Roger Lockyer edited the series before handing over to Clive Emsley (Professor of History at the Open University) and Gordon Martel (Professor of International History at the University of Northern British Columbia, Canada and Senior Research Fellow at De Montfort University).

MEDIEVAL ENGLAND

The Pre-Reformation Church in England 1400–1530 (Second edition)
Christopher Harper-Bill   0 582 28989 0

Lancastrians and Yorkists: The Wars of the Roses
David R Cook   0 582 35384 X

Family and Kinship in England 1450–1800
Will Coster   0 582 35717 9

TUDOR ENGLAND

Henry VII (Third edition)
Roger Lockyer & Andrew Thrush   0 582 20912 9

Henry VIII (Second edition)
M D Palmer   0 582 35437 4

Tudor Rebellions (Fourth edition)
Anthony Fletcher & Diarmaid MacCulloch   0 582 28990 4

The Reign of Mary I (Second edition)
Robert Tittler   0 582 06107 5

Early Tudor Parliaments 1485–1558
Michael A R Graves   0 582 03497 3

The English Reformation 1530–1570
W J Sheils   0 582 35398 X

Elizabethan Parliaments 1559–1601 (Second edition)
Michael A R Graves   0 582 29196 8

England and Europe 1485–1603 (Second edition)
Susan Doran   0 582 28991 2

The Church of England 1570–1640
Andrew Foster   0 582 35574 5

STUART BRITAIN

Social Change and Continuity: England 1550–1750 (Second edition)
Barry Coward   0 582 29442 8

James I (Second edition)
S J Houston   0 582 20911 0

The English Civil War 1640–1649
Martyn Bennett   0 582 35392 0

Charles I, 1625–1640
Brian Quintrell   0 582 00354 7

The English Republic 1649–1660 (Second edition)
Toby Barnard   0 582 08003 7

Radical Puritans in England 1550–1660
R J Acheson   0 582 35515 X

The Restoration and the England of Charles II (Second edition)
John Miller   0 582 29223 9

The Glorious Revolution (Second edition)
John Miller   0 582 29222 0

EARLY MODERN EUROPE

The Renaissance (Second edition)
Alison Brown   0 582 30781 3

The Emperor Charles V
Martyn Rady   0 582 35475 7

French Renaissance Monarchy: Francis I and Henry II (Second edition)
Robert Knecht   0 582 28707 3

The Protestant Reformation in Europe
Andrew Johnston   0 582 07020 1

The French Wars of Religion 1559–1598 (Second edition)
Robert Knecht   0 582 28533 X

Phillip II
Geoffrey Woodward   0 582 07232 8

The Thirty Years' War
Peter Limm   0 582 35373 4

Louis XIV
Peter Campbell   0 582 01770 X

Spain in the Seventeenth Century
Graham Darby   0 582 07234 4

Peter the Great
William Marshall   0 582 00355 5

EUROPE 1789–1918

Britain and the French Revolution
Clive Emsley 0 582 36961 4

Revolution and Terror in France 1789–1795 (Second edition)
D G Wright 0 582 00379 2

Napoleon and Europe
D G Wright 0 582 35457 9

The Abolition of Serfdom in Russia 1762–1907
David Moon 0 582 29486 X

Nineteenth-Century Russia: Opposition to Autocracy
Derek Offord 0 582 35767 5

The Constitutional Monarchy in France 1814–48
Pamela Pilbeam 0 582 31210 8

The 1848 Revolutions (Second edition)
Peter Jones 0 582 06106 7

The Italian Risorgimento
M Clark 0 582 00353 9

Bismarck & Germany 1862–1890 (Second edition)
D G Williamson 0 582 29321 9

Imperial Germany 1890–1918
Ian Porter, Ian Armour and Roger Lockyer 0 582 03496 5

The Dissolution of the Austro-Hungarian Empire 1867–1918 (Second edition)
John W Mason 0 582 29466 5

Second Empire and Commune: France 1848–1871 (Second edition)
William H C Smith 0 582 28705 7

France 1870–1914 (Second edition)
Robert Gildea 0 582 29221 2

The Scramble for Africa (Second edition)
M E Chamberlain 0 582 36881 2

Late Imperial Russia 1890–1917
John F Hutchinson 0 582 32721 0

The First World War
Stuart Robson 0 582 31556 5

Austria, Prussia and Germany 1806–1871
John Breuilly 0 582 43739 3

Napoleon: Conquest, Reform and Reorganisation
Clive Emsley 0 582 43795 4

The French Revolution 1787–1804
Peter Jones 0 582 77289 3

The Origins of the First World War (Third edition)
Gordon Martel 0 582 43804 7

EUROPE SINCE 1918

The Russian Revolution (Second edition)
Anthony Wood — 0 582 35559 1

Lenin's Revolution: Russia 1917–1921
David Marples — 0 582 31917 X

Stalin and Stalinism (Third edition)
Martin McCauley — 0 582 50587 9

The Weimar Republic (Second edition)
John Hiden — 0 582 28706 5

The Inter-War Crisis 1919–1939
Richard Overy — 0 582 35379 3

Fascism and the Right in Europe 1919–1945
Martin Blinkhorn — 0 582 07021 X

Spain's Civil War (Second edition)
Harry Browne — 0 582 28988 2

The Third Reich (Third edition)
D G Williamson — 0 582 20914 5

The Origins of the Second World War (Second edition)
R J Overy — 0 582 29085 6

The Second World War in Europe
Paul MacKenzie — 0 582 32692 3

The French at War 1934–1944
Nicholas Atkin — 0 582 36899 5

Anti-Semitism before the Holocaust
Albert S Lindemann — 0 582 36964 9

The Holocaust: The Third Reich and the Jews
David Engel — 0 582 32720 2

Germany from Defeat to Partition 1945–1963
D G Williamson — 0 582 29218 2

Britain and Europe since 1945
Alex May — 0 582 30778 3

Eastern Europe 1945–1969: From Stalinism to Stagnation
Ben Fowkes — 0 582 32693 1

Eastern Europe since 1970
Bülent Gökay — 0 582 32858 6

The Khrushchev Era 1953–1964
Martin McCauley — 0 582 27776 0

Hitler and the Rise of the Nazi Party
Frank McDonough — 0 582 50606 9

The Soviet Union Under Brezhnev
William Tompson — 0 582 32719 9

NINETEENTH-CENTURY BRITAIN

Britain before the Reform Acts: Politics and Society 1815–1832
Eric J Evans   0 582 00265 6

Parliamentary Reform in Britain c. 1770–1918
Eric J Evans   0 582 29467 3

Democracy and Reform 1815–1885
D G Wright   0 582 31400 3

Poverty and Poor Law Reform in Nineteenth-Century Britain 1834–1914:
From Chadwick to Booth
David Englander   0 582 31554 9

The Birth of Industrial Britain: Economic Change 1750–1850
Kenneth Morgan   0 582 29833 4

Chartism (Third edition)
Edward Royle   0 582 29080 5

Peel and the Conservative Party 1830–1850
Paul Adelman   0 582 35557 5

Gladstone, Disraeli and later Victorian Politics (Third edition)
Paul Adelman   0 582 29322 7

Britain and Ireland: From Home Rule to Independence
Jeremy Smith   0 582 30193 9

TWENTIETH-CENTURY BRITAIN

The Rise of the Labour Party 1880–1945 (Third edition)
Paul Adelman   0 582 29210 7

The Conservative Party and British Politics 1902–1951
Stuart Ball   0 582 08002 9

The Decline of the Liberal Party 1910–1931 (Second edition)
Paul Adelman   0 582 27733 7

The British Women's Suffrage Campaign 1866–1928
Harold L Smith   0 582 29811 3

War & Society in Britain 1899–1948
Rex Pope   0 582 03531 7

The British Economy since 1914: A Study in Decline?
Rex Pope   0 582 30194 7

Unemployment in Britain between the Wars
Stephen Constantine   0 582 35232 0

The Attlee Governments 1945–1951
Kevin Jefferys   0 582 06105 9

The Conservative Governments 1951–1964
Andrew Boxer   0 582 20913 7

Britain under Thatcher
Anthony Seldon and Daniel Collings   0 582 31714 2

Britain and Empire 1880–1945
Dane Kennedy   0 582 41493 8

INTERNATIONAL HISTORY

The Eastern Question 1774–1923 (Second edition)
A L Macfie   0 582 29195 X

India 1885–1947: The Unmaking of an Empire
Ian Copland   0 582 38173 8

The United States and the First World War
Jennifer D Keene   0 582 35620 2

Women and the First World War
Susan R Grayzel   0 582 41876 3

Anti-Semitism before the Holocaust
Albert S Lindemann   0 582 36964 9

The Origins of the Cold War 1941–1949 (Third edition)
Martin McCauley   0 582 77284 2

Russia, America and the Cold War 1949–1991
Martin McCauley   0 582 27936 4

The Arab–Israeli Conflict
Kirsten E Schulze   0 582 31646 4

The United Nations since 1945: Peacekeeping and the Cold War
Norrie MacQueen   0 582 35673 3

Decolonisation: The British Experience since 1945
Nicholas J White   0 582 29087 2

WORLD HISTORY

China in Transformation 1900–1949
Colin Mackerras   0 582 31209 4

Japan Faces the World 1925–1952
Mary L Hanneman   0 582 36898 7

Japan in Transformation 1952–2000
Jeff Kingston   0 582 41875 5

China since 1949
Linda Benson   0 582 35722 5

US HISTORY

American Abolitionists
Stanley Harrold   0 582 35738 1

The American Civil War 1861–1865
Reid Mitchell   0 582 31973 0

America in the Progressive Era 1890–1914
Lewis L Gould   0 582 35671 7

The United States and the First World War
Jennifer D Keene   0 582 35620 2

The Truman Years 1945–1953
Mark S Byrnes   0 582 32904 3

The Korean War
Steven Hugh Lee   0 582 31988 9

The Origins of the Vietnam War
Fredrik Logevall   0 582 31918 8

The Vietnam War
Mitchell Hall   0 582 32859 4

American Expansionism 1783–1860
Mark S Joy   0 582 36965 7

The United States and Europe in the Twentieth Century
David Ryan   0 582 30864 X

The Civil Rights Movement
Bruce J. Dierenfield   0 582 35737 3